Building Resilient Pathways

A Guide for Job Coaches

Maria Smith

The Rural
Publishing Company

First published by The Rural Publishing Company 2025.

Print (Paperback): 978-1-923008-45-8
eBook: 978-1-923008-46-5

The Rural Publishing Company
Website: https://theruralpublishingcompany.com.au
Email: hello@theruralpublishingcompany.com.au

Contents

Contents

Dedication

To my son Lucas, who is truly his namesake to me.

Lucas: Latin from 'lux,' meaning light; the bringer of light.

Part 1

Laying the Foundation for Transformation

Welcome to Building Resilient Pathways. This book has been a passion project, and I'm excited to share the skills and knowledge I've developed over the years with everyone working in employment services.

After completing my Master's of Applied Positive Psychology (MAPP) in 2023, I knew that I needed to write a book that would expand on my research and have a practical and influential impact on the sector's frontline.

My capstone project was based on Hope Theory (Snyder, 2002)[1] and its application in supporting individuals facing long-term unemployment.

Hope Theory is an incredibly powerful, evidence-based model that can be highly effective in a coaching context.

But before we can activate hope in others, we must first cultivate it within ourselves.

Part 1 of Building Resilient Pathways focuses on establishing the internal foundation that enables you to coach with clarity, compassion and conviction. Understanding your emotional landscape, values, strengths and the energy you bring into every interaction will make you a highly effective job coach.

This section is not about strategies or systems. It is about presence. It is about becoming more aware of who you are, how you think and what drives you. Because the truth is, your way of being matters just as much as your coaching techniques. The energy you carry, the beliefs you hold and the emotional awareness you develop all shape the experience your clients have with you.

You will explore the power of self-awareness and learn how to pause, reflect and tune into your thoughts and emotions so you can respond with intention rather than reaction. You will discover how self-awareness is not just a skill, but a way of being that transforms your coaching from transactional to relational.

Uncovering what truly matters to you and how to align your work with those values, and learning how to identify and leverage your energising strengths so you can coach from a place of authenticity and vitality.

The three E's of coaching are linked to Hope Theory and the Hope Activation Framework, demonstrating how emotion, energy and empathy shape every interaction you have with your clients. You will learn how to manage emotional labour, protect your energy and cultivate empathy without burning out. You will discover how to bring ten-out-of-ten energy into your sessions, even on the days when you feel like a three.

Before we dive in, I want to be open and honest with you. You might encounter some resistance on your coaching journey – both from within and from the demanding pace of your professional life. This work requires honesty, vulnerability and a willingness to grow. But it is also deeply rewarding. Knowing yourself allows you to connect more deeply with others. When you understand your values, you can coach with integrity, and when you manage your energy, you can sustain your impact.

Storytelling is the most powerful way to learn about human behaviour because it's based on people's experiences. This book includes stories about job coaches and clients (whose names have been changed for privacy) I've worked with over the years – their experiences will likely resonate with you. I'm also a big fan of metaphors and analogies, so you'll see plenty of them scattered throughout the book.

Through real-world examples and relatable anecdotes, I'll help you discover how coaching skills can be cultivated in the moments between moments – in the brief pauses of reflection scattered throughout your day.

Part 1 is your foundation. The inner work you do now will prepare you for the outer work of activating hope in others. When you build the emotional resilience and insight needed to hold space for your clients, you'll learn to bring your best self into every coaching conversation.

So, take a breath. Settle in. This is your opportunity to reconnect with your purpose, rediscover your strengths and realign with what truly matters. Because when you show up with clarity, compassion and conviction, you become the spark that helps others believe in their future.

And that is where transformation begins.

Chapter One

Coaching with Clarity

The Power of
Self-Awareness

*I met Alex a few years ago in a training program I was
delivering for a local employment provider. Despite his
experience as a consultant, he often sensed something
was missing from his coaching practice. At times, he felt
frustrated with some of his clients, particularly the quiet
ones who seemed unmotivated or disengaged. Alex would
spend sessions making suggestions and plans to push
clients to take action, often with little success.*

*During a particularly challenging session, Alex realised he
had offered multiple solutions to a client, and they still
seemed completely disconnected. Finally, the client spoke
up and said, 'None of those things interest me. You don't
understand what matters to me.'*

The comment stopped Alex in his tracks. For someone who always felt he had the answers, he couldn't find the words to respond. Could it be that he was part of the problem? He wasn't truly listening or connecting. He was busy ticking off tasks and filling the silences with solutions, but not truly understanding his clients.

In that moment, he recognised it was time to turn the lens inward …

Over my years working in employment services, I've heard stories like this more times than I can count. There's no doubt about the challenges we face in the industry. Achieving positive employment outcomes takes time and energy. When the pressure to meet targets and stay on top of increasing case loads becomes overwhelming, it can feel like an overwhelming place to be.

But there's something special about the work you do and the support you provide to your clients. They often come to you at times in their lives when they're at their most vulnerable, hoping someone can steer them in a different direction.

The role you have in helping them is rewarding and demanding at the same time. I know that amidst the whirlwind of your daily responsibilities, cultivating self-awareness seems like a luxury, not a necessity. However, self-awareness is a crucial skill that you need to possess. Without it, navigating challenges could be harder than it needs to be.

Imagine for a moment the profound impact that a deepened sense of self could have on your work. Self-awareness is not just a tool. It is the essence that can transform your coaching from effective to extraordinary. Think of it like a silent, powerful current beneath the surface, shaping every interaction, piece of advice and moment of connection with those you aim to uplift.

To develop self-awareness, you need to pause, reflect and turn the lens inward to explore *your* inner world. The more you know about yourself, the more successful you'll be. When you understand how self-awareness underpins the level of impact you have as a coach, it will bring a new sense of satisfaction and joy to your work.

Self-awareness is the key that unlocks insights and wisdom, allowing you to navigate the complexities of human emotions and behaviours with grace and precision. Serving as your compass, self-awareness will guide you to the heart of your client's challenges, enabling you to offer empathetic and individualised support.

I promise that the time you invest in developing your self-awareness will result in deeper connections, more effective coaching and a renewed sense of purpose in your work.

> *'Knowing others is intelligence; knowing yourself is true wisdom.'*
>
> Lao Tzu

Imagine self-awareness as a lighthouse guiding you through the foggy waters of biases and emotions. The beacon illuminates a path, ensuring you do not lose sight of your true purpose – to empower and uplift your clients. For you as a job coach, this journey is not just about honing your skills but about deeply embedding the wisdom gained through all of life's experiences and channelling it into your practice.

But what does this look like in the real world? Consider a seasoned job coach who notices her tendency to fill silences with advice rather than allowing her clients the space to find their own answers. With self-awareness, she catches herself in the moment. Instead, she poses a question that sparks a moment of clarity for her client. This subtle shift in awareness transforms the coaching session from a one-way dialogue to a collaborative journey of discovery.

The path to self-awareness is not without its challenges. It can be confronting to shine a light on our vulnerabilities and acknowledge the areas where we fall short. However, when we face challenges head-on, growth occurs. By embracing practices such as journaling, mindfulness and seeking feedback, coaches can turn these challenges into stepping stones toward greater self-knowledge and effectiveness. We'll explore these specific strategies in more detail throughout Part One.

Building the foundation of emotional intelligence

You've probably heard of Emotional Intelligence (EI). Made famous by psychologist Daniel Goleman[2], EI is all about recognising and managing our emotions and the emotions of others. Goleman's work has changed how we think about intelligence and its role in achieving personal and professional success.

Emotional Intelligence (EI) has five essential elements:

- Self-awareness

- Self-regulation

- Motivation

- Empathy

- Social skills

These tools are essential for navigating your emotions and social interactions smoothly. Combining emotional intelligence with coaching can significantly enhance the coach-client relationship. Job coaches with high EI comprehend their clients' emotional landscapes and respond with thoughtfulness and empathy. The ability aids in designing strategies tailored to the client's needs and emotions. Job coaches who understand emotions well can see their clients' feelings and respond with care. The skill helps create coaching plans that fit clients' needs and emotions, making sessions more effective and transformative and enhancing the job coach-client relationship.

Research has consistently shown that EI is vital for success across various aspects of life, including professional and personal relationships. According to Talent Smart research[3], emotional intelligence accounts for 58% of job performance. Additionally, individuals with higher EI earn more annually than those with lower EI, highlighting its influence on career success and financial wellbeing.

Enhancing your emotional intelligence allows you to connect with your clients more profoundly, communicate more effectively, and foster a collaborative coaching atmosphere that promotes growth and development.

> *'Emotional intelligence is the key to both personal and professional success.'*
>
> Daniel Goleman

Self-Awareness

Frequently regarded as the foundation of emotional intelligence, self-awareness focuses on understanding your emotions, strengths, weaknesses, values and motivations. Those who are genuinely self-aware can see how their feelings influence their thoughts, actions and overall performance. They tend to be introspective and are deeply connected to their inner emotional world.

Key Points of Self-Awareness:

- Emotional self-awareness: the ability to recognise and understand your emotions for better emotional management.

- Accurate self-assessment: evaluating your strengths and limits is crucial for personal and professional growth.

- Self-confidence: a solid sense of your value and abilities empowers you to tackle challenges assuredly.

Now is a good opportunity for you to reflect.

How self-aware are you?

Can you recognise your emotions and put a name on them when they arise?

Do you know when you're working within your strengths?

What do you believe about yourself and your ability to be a highly effective job coach?

'Self-awareness is the ability to take an honest look at your life without any attachment to it being right or wrong, good or bad.'

Debbie Ford

Self-Regulation

Mastering self-regulation means taking control of your emotions with ease. Imagine managing stress effortlessly and maintaining your composure even in the most challenging circumstances. Self-regulation helps curb impulsive reactions and craft thoughtful responses to enhance adaptability and resilience. By practising self-regulation, you equip yourself to handle life's highs and lows with elegance and composure.

Key points of self-regulation:

- Emotional control: is managing your emotions and impulses effectively.

- Trustworthiness: is adhering to honest and ethical standards.

- Conscientiousness: is taking responsibility for

your performance.

- Adaptability: is being flexible in response to change and challenges.

- Innovation: is embracing new ideas and methods.

Can you think of a time when you've struggled to control your emotional response to a situation or experience? Are you able to recognise when you're not performing at your best?

Self-regulation is a critical skill for you to develop, and with conscious practice, you can become highly effective at it.

Motivation

Motivation is a component of Daniel Goleman's Emotional Intelligence framework, functioning as the catalyst that helps individuals work towards their goals and aspirations. Your inner passion for success extends beyond external rewards, reflecting a commitment to excel, grow, and persist despite challenges.

Embracing intrinsic motivation is essential for anyone seeking their full potential.

Key points of motivation:

- Achievement drive: means trying to do your best. People with drive set high goals and work hard to meet them. They like feedback and always look for ways to improve.

- Commitment: means caring about your work and being dedicated to doing it well. It involves finding meaning in your job and maintaining high standards.

- Initiative: people with initiative are proactive. They don't wait for things to happen – they take action to make things happen by tackling challenges and seizing opportunities.

- Optimism: is the belief that you can achieve your goals despite setbacks. A positive attitude helps you bounce back from failures and keep moving forward.

With these powerful motivation strategies, you can tackle challenges and maintain your composure.

So, let me ask you – how motivated are you?

Empathy

Empathy is a game-changer in coaching and career development. It's all about understanding and sharing the feelings of others and showing genuine concern for their wellbeing. Empathy helps job coaches connect more deeply with their clients, creating a supportive atmosphere where individuals feel genuinely heard and valued.

You can better grasp your clients' needs and motivations when you are empathetic. This understanding allows you to offer personalised guidance and support. By demonstrating empathy, you'll be able to establish trust and rapport, which is essential to a successful coaching relationship.

Empathy encourages open communication, helping clients clearly express their goals and dreams. Empathetic coaches provide constructive feedback and encouragement, assisting clients to bounce back from setbacks and stay committed to their growth.

Simply put, empathy is a must-have skill. It's the foundation for deeper, more effective coaching interactions. It creates an environment where your clients can thrive and reach their full potential.

Social Skills

Social skills are crucial for job coaches who want to build a strong rapport with their clients. These five skills help you communicate well, manage relationships, and easily navigate your social networks.

Effective communication

Good communication is vital. As a job coach, you need to be clear when you talk and listen carefully. This means expressing ideas and giving feedback in a way that your clients understand and showing that you really hear what they are saying. Getting better at communication helps you connect more deeply and support clients better.

Conflict resolution

Dealing with conflicts is another big part of social skills. Great job coaches know how to handle disagreements and help clients solve problems at work. By staying calm and fair, you can guide your clients to find helpful solutions, strengthen your relationship and create a positive environment.

Building rapport

Building rapport, or a good connection, is crucial for gaining trust and respect from clients. Job coaches can do this by showing genuine interest in their clients' lives, understanding their feelings, and always being there for them. When clients feel understood, they are more likely to engage with you fully and achieve their goals.

Influence and leadership

Being able to influence and lead is also essential for job coaches. If you share a clear vision and believe in your clients' abilities, you can inspire them to take bold steps toward their goals. Setting a positive example can help your clients find direction and purpose in their careers.

Teamwork and collaboration

Working well with others and being a team player are also important social skills that job coaches need. By showing how to collaborate and support each other, you can show clients how to thrive in a team setting, making their work lives more fulfilling and productive.

We will unpack these specific skills in further detail in the next few chapters and show you how to use tools to enhance your coaching ability.

Self-awareness is the basis of your coaching practice and the driving force behind your clients' transformation. When you master the art of understanding yourself, you'll be able to connect more deeply with others. Building self-awareness is a professional and personal commitment to excellence in service to our most vulnerable people in society.

So, let's dive in and add some tools to your toolbox.

Practical Tool: The Reflective Practice Model

In their work *'Reflective Practice for Coaches and Clients: An Integrated Model for Learning,'* Thomas Tkach presents an integrated *Reflective Practice Model*[4].

The model demonstrates the effectiveness of reflection, awareness and self-regulation as developmental tools for job coaches. The research provides a blueprint for understanding how these self-processing mechanisms enhance learning, promote growth and improve performance.

Reflective practice is vital for continuous learning and growth. The *Reflective Practice Model* encourages a cycle of self-observation and self-evaluation. Using this model will give you insight into your actions and behaviours and the triggers they create within yourself and your clients. The model is about continuously addressing specific problems and refining your skills.

The Reflective Practice Model encompasses Schön's concept of Reflection-on-Action, which involves building on previous learning and linking it to current and future practice[5]. You can make positive changes by taking a step back from your coaching, evaluating it and extracting meaning.

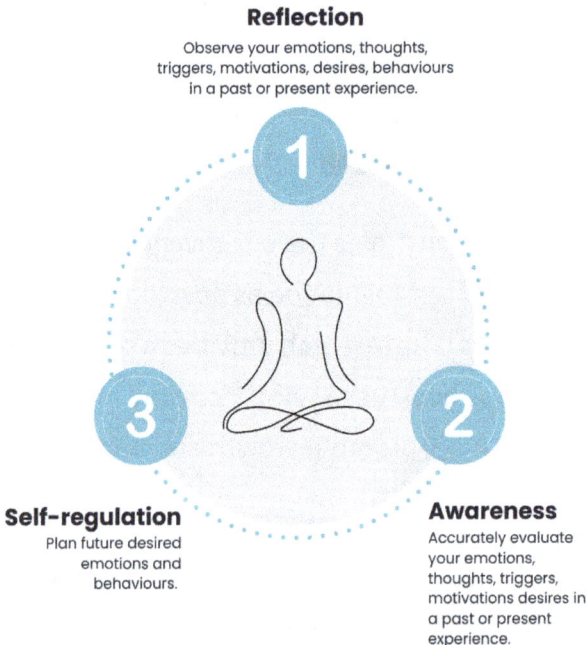

Reflection
Observe your emotions, thoughts, triggers, motivations, desires, behaviours in a past or present experience.

1

3

2

Self-regulation
Plan future desired emotions and behaviours.

Awareness
Accurately evaluate your emotions, thoughts, triggers, motivations desires in a past or present experience.

The Reflective Practice Model

When you integrate reflective practice into your work, it will enhance your coaching effectiveness. You'll uncover the assumptions, beliefs and thought patterns that influence your actions and ultimately impact the outcomes you get with your clients. Reflective practice will help you stay rational, composed and grounded in your communication.

A mountain of evidence demonstrates how reflective practice is an essential tool for coaches. It forms the backbone of developing deep and meaningful connections, fostering self-acceptance and confidence, and creating an environment conducive to challenging work.

Julia Carden, Rebecca J. Jones, and Jonathan Passmore conducted a mixed-methods study published in *Current Psychology* exploring the benefits of reflective practice to build self-awareness[6]. They found that the key enablers to better self-awareness include experiential learning supported by reflection in a psychologically safe environment.

My experience backs this research. I use reflective practice regularly, and it makes me a far more competent and skilled coach.

Coach's insight: Alex's breakthrough

Determined to improve his sessions, Alex recognised that he needed to change how he worked with his clients. Alex called me a few weeks after the training session and he shared his experiences with me. I suggested he start a reflective journal to document how sessions were going, what was working and what behaviours he noticed he was doing. The practice revealed a pattern – a tendency to keep sessions moving by filling silences with advice rather than allowing clients the time and space to share their thoughts and feelings.

One afternoon, during a session with a client named Jamie, who was struggling with a work-related decision, Alex caught himself and paused before offering suggestions. Instead, he took a deep breath and asked, 'What do you think would make you happiest in your job?' This simple question sparked a significant revelation for Jamie, who shared her passion for helping people. At that moment, Alex realised the power of curiosity and asking questions instead of giving advice and instructing his clients on what to do.

Together, Alex and Jamie explored options and discussed pathways, including training opportunities and employment goals. Within weeks, Jamie enrolled in a certificate course in community services and was volunteering at a local community house. Through Alex's support, Jamie found a job as a home care support worker and plans to do further training.

Following this positive experience, Alex noticed a profound shift as he continued to integrate self-awareness into his coaching practice, utilising the Reflective Practice Model. Sessions became more collaborative, and clients felt empowered to explore solutions. Alex's newfound self-awareness enhanced his coaching effectiveness and deepened his connections with clients.

Through these client interactions, Alex learned that self-awareness is not a destination but a continuous growth process. By embracing the ongoing journey of self-improvement, Alex transformed his coaching practice from effective to extraordinary.

Applying reflective practice in coaching

You can apply reflective practice using various methods and techniques to help you reflect on your experiences and actions. This continuous learning process enables you to recognise the patterns shaping your thinking and action, ultimately enhancing your coaching effectiveness.

Keep a reflective journal: Journaling is an excellent way to enhance self-awareness by recording your thoughts, feelings, and experiences from client coaching sessions. This practice can help you identify patterns in your behaviour and emotional responses.

Seek feedback and self-assess: Regularly ask for feedback from colleagues or mentors and reflect on your client sessions. Feedback will provide you with different perspectives and help you improve your practice.

Reflective questions:

After your sessions, ask yourself the following questions:

- What went well?

- What would I do differently next time?

- What action can I take now based on this reflection?

Remember Job Coach Alex? He used reflective practice as a tool and journaled his thoughts and behaviours after each client appointment. He had three standard questions he asked himself each time and used these as prompts to unpack his challenges with particular clients. This is where he identified the patterns around his behaviours that were, in fact, the barriers to some of his clients moving forward.

Understanding our view of the world

To build self-awareness, you need to understand how your perceptions, projections and beliefs impact your thoughts, emotions and behaviours. These three elements shape how we interpret the world and interact with others.

Perceptions are the unique lenses through which we view the world. They are shaped by our past experiences, cultural background and personal biases. Imagine wearing glasses that tint everything blue – this would be your perception, altering how you see every detail.

Projections are the unconscious act of transferring our feelings, desires or thoughts onto others. Picture yourself as a projector, casting your insecurities or hopes onto the blank screen of your client's lives.

As a job coach, recognising how your perceptions and projections influence your view of a client's situation is critical. For instance, if you feel anxious about a client's job prospects, you may unconsciously communicate your anxiety to them, which can affect their confidence and motivation.

Think about your clients and your expectations of them. Do you believe they will never find a job? Are you limiting them by your low expectations? There is a difference between their lack of skill and experience and your lack of belief in them. Depending on your beliefs, this can affect the outcome.

Ideally, your role as a job coach is to project your confidence and belief in their abilities and inspire them to see new possibilities and take bold steps forward.

What do you believe?

Beliefs are the quiet architects of your coaching practice. When I mention beliefs, I'm not referring to your stance on religion or politics but the subtle whispers you tell yourself that often go unnoticed. As a coach, I know these personal mantras shape every outcome in client interactions. Negative or unresourceful beliefs can cast long shadows, influencing your effectiveness and the relationships you build. It's crucial to clear the path for positive beliefs that will guide you towards the extraordinary future you and your clients deserve.

Understanding and transforming the beliefs that hold you back is a pivotal part of the journey.

Imagine if you believed you weren't knowledgeable enough to provide valuable coaching. A message like this could form a belief that you're not good enough. Or if you were nervous about meeting new clients, believing you might not be able to connect with them. This might lead you to doubt your ability to make a significant impact. Perhaps you lack the authority or confidence to guide someone towards their career goals, making you hesitant to assert your expertise.

These ingrained beliefs influence how you connect with and influence others. It's essential to nurture beliefs that support the life and career you envision for yourself and your clients. Consider your coaching practice. What empowering beliefs must you adopt to achieve success? If you aspire to be a transformative coach, scrutinise and replace limiting beliefs, such as *'I don't have the expertise'* or *'I might fail,'* with affirmations like *'I am knowledgeable and constantly learning'* and *'I am confident in my ability to help my clients succeed.'*

Empowerment is the cornerstone of cultivating positive beliefs. By doing so, you will pave the way to an inspiring and successful coaching practice, transforming your client's dreams into reality.

Activity: Practising personal reflection

Reflect regularly to gain insight into your perceptions, projections and beliefs. Reflective practice can help you become more aware of how these elements influence your thoughts, behaviours and interactions.

One effective method is journaling. By regularly documenting your thoughts, feelings and experiences, you can gain deeper insights into your beliefs and how they shape your coaching practice. Journaling allows you to consciously examine recurring themes, identify limiting beliefs and explore new perspectives. It provides a safe space to process your emotions and track your progress over time.

Consider setting aside a few minutes each day to write about your interactions with clients, your wins, and any challenges you face. Reflect on the beliefs that surface during these moments and how they influence your behaviour.

Here are some prompts to help you start reflecting:

- *'What do I believe about my abilities as a coach?'*

- *'How do my current beliefs support or hinder my success?'*

- *'What past experiences have shaped my beliefs about my coaching abilities?'*

- *'How do my beliefs about success influence my actions and decisions?'*

- *'What new beliefs do I need to cultivate to achieve my coaching goals?'*

Incorporate journaling daily to boost self-awareness and personal growth. This approach enhances your understanding of yourself and empowers you to navigate your life with greater clarity and confidence.

Like job coach Alex, you have the ability to change your thoughts and behaviours, using reflective practice. I like journaling because writing down your thoughts creates the space and distance needed to reflect on what has happened, where we are, and what is ahead. Looking at thoughts rather than being consumed by them allows us to separate the need to accept our feelings and commit to the changes we need to make.

You might prefer to seek out feedback or discuss your reflections with a trusted colleague or use mindfulness as part of your reflective practice. There's no right or wrong way to practice self-reflection.

Actionable reflections

At the end of each chapter, you'll find these actionable reflection points. They are designed to give you a quick summary of the content covered and prompt you to take action.

- Employment services staff face challenges like uncertainty and being overwhelmed, making self-awareness even more crucial, so don't dismiss its importance.

- Self-awareness is essential for effective coaching, transforming it from good to extraordinary – work on developing this.

- Developing self-awareness involves practices like journaling, mindfulness and seeking feedback. Which one will you adopt to start your self-awareness journey?

- The Reflective Practice Model helps coaches gain

insights into their actions and improve their effectiveness. What questions will you regularly reflect on as part of your practice?

- Continuous growth in self-awareness is vital for ongoing improvement in coaching practice, and remember to take small steps forward. Rome wasn't built in a day.

Conclusion: Take your first step forward

As you walk down the path of transforming lives, remember that the journey begins within. By diving deep into your perceptions, projections and beliefs, you can unlock the potential to connect deeply with your clients. Imagine yourself as an explorer, charting the intricate landscape of your personality and discovering hidden gems of insight that will ultimately illuminate the path for your clients.

Embrace self-awareness and self-reflection as your trusted companions. Regularly polish the lens through which you view the world, ensuring it remains clear and unbiased. Understanding your inner self allows you to guide your clients clearly and powerfully, inspiring their self-discovery and growth.

Every step you take towards understanding yourself creates a ripple effect, empowering your clients to challenge their own limiting beliefs and embrace new, empowering ones. Together, you will create space for transformation where dreams and potential are realised.

Now that you've taken this first step, there's no going back. In fact, the journey is only going to get better from here! We'll continue to explore who you are and what drives you as a coach, by unpacking your strengths and values in the next chapter.

Chapter Two

Embracing Values and Strengths

'I thought this was what I wanted to do. But now I'm not so sure.'

Sarah, Job Coach

Sarah, a job coach from an employment provider, shared this with me during a break at a session I was delivering at her workplace.

She was passionate about her job and deeply valued caring for others and making a difference in their lives. However, she struggled with the constant pressure of meeting KPIs and targets for job placements. The stress was taking a toll on her motivation and engagement. So much so that she was seriously considering whether the job was a good fit for her. There were too many conflicting tasks, making it hard for her to find meaning and purpose in both the work she was required to do and the work she loved to do. She wanted to find a balance between the aspects of the job that she truly enjoyed and the tasks that drained her energy and eroded her motivation. But it felt too hard, and she was ready to give up ...

Have you ever taken a moment to think about what truly matters to you?

It's such an eye-opening experience to pause and reflect on what you genuinely care about. Sometimes, it can be a bit tricky to pinpoint exactly what drives us, but it's worth the effort. Your life is a beautiful reflection of your values and what matters most to you. These values shape your decisions, define what you love, and set the boundaries for what you cannot tolerate. And guess what? Everyone has values, even if you haven't consciously recognised them yet.

Values are deeply embedded in our emotions, and they are the feelings we seek to experience. For instance, if owning a car is important to you, it might be because it gives you a sense of freedom and independence. In this case, your core values are freedom and independence.

Similarly, you might value your job for the pay cheque and the sense of security and comfort it provides. Or perhaps you love your job because you make a difference in helping people.

Understanding your values is like unlocking the blueprint of your decision-making process. It offers profound insights into why you make the choices you do. When you grasp what you truly value, you can align your actions to create the future you desire.

Imagine you're standing at a crossroads, and each direction represents a different value. One path might lead to adventure and excitement, while another offers stability and security. By understanding your values, you can confidently choose the path that aligns with your true self. It's like having a personal compass guiding you towards a fulfilling and meaningful life.

Before I had my son, I valued freedom and adventure. I lived overseas and enjoyed my independence. Once I had my son, providing for him became a priority, so the value of security took precedence over freedom and adventure. This changed my momentum, and it's the reason I started my company, Bounce, to provide a future for my son.

*'Values are the gateway to your most
authentic self.'*

Shannah Kennedy

Understanding how values impact your life is
transformative. When two people share the same values,
they have a better chance of staying together. If a past
relationship failed, it might be due to a values shift.
For example, you might have valued spontaneity and
adventure when you were younger. As you mature, you
value reliability and security, but your partner sees this
as predictable and boring, and they miss the person you
were when you first met. It's easy to see how breakdowns
can arise.

This concept also applies to your professional
life. Understanding how values influence decisions
empowers you to align with them. Gaining awareness of
what you value in a career allows you to look for jobs and
employers with similar values.

Reflect on your previous jobs. You might have started a
job with high hopes, believing the environment aligned
with your values, only to realise later that your workplace
or managers' values clashed with yours. Or perhaps

you've chosen job security over relocating to pursue better opportunities or further education, because it felt more comfortable and stable.

The key takeaway is that understanding the impact of your values and how they manifest is life-changing. Are you having that a-ha moment? This is powerful stuff that can transform your life. Evaluate your values in every aspect of your life. If your vision isn't materialising, it's likely because your values aren't being met. You don't have to make changes immediately. Just recognise and accept how your values influence your life.

Coach's insight: Sarah's breakthrough

Sarah and I caught up again a few weeks after our first conversation, and I asked her to reflect on her core values. At first, she wasn't sure exactly what I was talking about. She told me that her family and friends were important to her, along with her home, and that she volunteered at a community food bank twice a week. I explained to Sarah that these values are what I call 'means values' – things that we have or experience. What we want to understand are our 'end values', otherwise known as the feeling that we get from having something or experiencing something.

We went through an exercise to identify what truly mattered to her, both personally and professionally. It became clear that her core values, or the 'feelings' she loved to experience, included caring, making a difference and helping others.

With this newfound clarity, we brainstormed ways to align her daily tasks with her core values. Instead of focusing solely on the numbers, Sarah started to see each job placement as an opportunity to make a meaningful impact on someone's life. She began approaching her work with a renewed sense of purpose, viewing each interaction as a chance to care for and support her clients.

We also discussed how Sarah could effectively communicate her values to her team and supervisor. By sharing her passion for making a difference, she was able to foster a more supportive and understanding work environment. Her colleagues began to appreciate the importance of her values and supported her in finding creative solutions to meet targets without compromising her principles.

The transformation was remarkable. Sarah's engagement and motivation soared, and she started to achieve her KPIs more consistently. She found deeper fulfilment and satisfaction by aligning her work with her core values. Her clients also benefited from her renewed energy and dedication, leading to more successful job placements.

This story highlights the power of understanding and prioritising your values. When you align your actions with what truly matters to you, it enhances your professional performance and brings a profound sense of personal satisfaction. So, take the time to discover your values and let them guide you on your journey. You might be surprised at the positive changes that follow.

Take a moment to reflect on your values and how they influence your decisions. Think about the moments when you felt truly fulfilled and satisfied.

- What were you doing?

- Who were you with?

- What values were you honouring in those moments?

These experiences can provide valuable clues about your core values. And remember, this is an ongoing process. As you grow and evolve, your values may shift. Regularly revisiting and reassessing your values can help you stay aligned with what matters most. So, are you ready to discover what truly drives you and start living a life that reflects your deepest values?

Activity: Discovering and prioritising your core values

Identifying your core values is a journey of self-discovery that can be both enlightening and empowering. Here are some steps to help you uncover what truly matters to you:

1. Reflect on your experiences: Think about moments in your life when you felt truly fulfilled and satisfied. What were you doing? Who were you with? What values were you honouring in those moments? These experiences can provide clues about your core values.

2. Consider your role models: Reflect on the people you admire and respect. What qualities do they possess that you find inspiring? These qualities often align with your values.

3. Evaluate your decisions: Look at the choices you've made, both big and small. What motivated those decisions? What values were

BUILDING RESILIENT PATHWAYS

you prioritising? Understanding the reasons behind your choices can help you identify your core values.

4. Identify what you dislike: Sometimes, knowing what you don't value can be just as revealing as knowing what you do. Think about situations or behaviours that you find intolerable. The opposite of these can often point to your core values.

5. Use a values list: Reviewing a list of common values can help you identify which resonates with you. For example, values like achievement, creativity, independence and security might stand out to you. Choose the ones that feel most important and meaningful.

6. Ask yourself questions: Reflect on questions like:

What makes me feel happy and fulfilled?
What do I want to achieve in my life?
What principles guide my actions and decisions?
What do I want to be remembered for?

7. Prioritise your values: Once you've identified a list of potential values, prioritise them.

Determine which ones are most important to you and why. This can help you focus on what truly matters.

8. Test your values: Put your values into practice and see how they feel. Do they align with your actions and decisions? Are they helping you live a more fulfilling life? Adjust as needed to ensure your values accurately reflect who you are.

Let's explore number 5 – The Values List. In this activity, you'll explore two lists of feeling values: one for your life in general and another for your career. Take the time to reflect on the values that resonate most with you in each category.

The Values List

What do you value most in life?

Pick 10 values that are important to you in life:

☐ Achievement

☐ Affiliation

☐ Challenge

☐ Creativity

☐ Entrepreneurism

☐ Financial success

☐ Helping others

☐ Independence

☐ Initiative

☐ Integrity

☐ Leadership

☐ Organisation

☐ Personal development

☐ Professional development

☐ Recognition/prestige

☐ Security

☐ Structure

☐ Variety

☐ Love

☐ Growth

☐ Contribution

☐ Adventure

☐ Passion

☐ Happiness

☐ Intelligence

☐ Approval

☐ Success

☐ Health

☐ Acceptance

☐ Making a difference

☐ Belonging

Other_____

What do you value most in career/work?

☐ Achievement

☐ Affiliation

☐ Challenge

☐ Creativity

☐ Entrepreneurism

☐ Financial success

☐ Helping others

☐ Independence

☐ Initiative

☐ Integrity

☐ Leadership

☐ Organisation

☐ Personal development

☐ Professional development

☐ Recognition/prestige

☐ Security

☐ Structure

☐ Variety

☐ Love

☐ Growth

☐ Contribution

☐ Adventure

☐ Passion

☐ Happiness

☐ Intelligence

☐ Approval

☐ Success

☐ Health

☐ Acceptance

☐ Making a difference

☐ Belonging

Other_____

Now, let's take the top three values from each list and ask yourself these questions:

- What's important to me about this value?

- What does this value give me?

- What do I gain when this value is met?

- Why does this value hold significance for me? Is it a belief passed down from my family, or is it based on an experience where I was rewarded for a certain behaviour?

Life Values

Take the top 3 values from your life list and explain why each one is important to you.

For example, if you chose security, you might say, 'Security is important to me because it means my life will be financially stable and I can support my children.'

Life Value #1: _____

What is important to you about this value?

Life Value #2: _____

What is important to you about this value?

Life Value #3: _____

What is important to you about this value?

Career/Work Values

Take the top 3 values from your career list and explain why each one is important to you.

For example, if you chose Approval, you might say, 'Approval is important to me because, without it, I feel like I am not doing a good enough job, which makes me feel uneasy at work.'

Career/Work Value #1: _____

What is important to you about this value?

Career/Work Value #2: _____

What is important to you about this value?

Career/Work Value #3: _____

What is important to you about this value?

Remember to revisit the entire list periodically. This practice will help you explore value conflicts in the future and equip you with the tools you need in any situation.

'The things you are passionate about are not random. They are your calling.'

Fabienne Fredrickson

Embracing your strengths

When you take the time to reflect on your strengths, you're not just improving your wellbeing, productivity and performance; you're unlocking the potential that can transform your work experience. As a job coach, you know how important it is to help others find their path, but it's equally crucial to recognise and harness your strengths.

Finding out what strengths you have can be daunting and hard to recognise. I always like to start by asking myself a few key questions:

- What energises me or gives me energy when I am doing it?

- What motivates and gets me going for the day?

- What excites me? What do I love talking about and why?

- What are the tasks or things I move quickly through, or what are the tasks or things that I find easy to do?

These questions are a great start in identifying your realised or unrealised strengths. Your realised or unrealised strengths are the essence of who you are, and your identity is often wrapped up in them. Realised or unrealised strengths feel comfortable, feel good, ring true, sound right, look good or right. They paint a picture of who you are at your core. They are simply energising.

When identifying your strengths, be mindful of your learned behaviours. These are tasks or things that you perform well and have learned over time. However, they can be de-energising when you're working in them, particularly for a long time. For example, you might be good at working with detail, but if you were to work on it all day, every day, you might lose energy and motivation quickly. Those with detail as a realised strength love being in it, they thrive on it and can't wait to dive in.

Mix up your work to manage the de-energising factor of your learned behaviours. Move into something more energising when you notice you're losing steam or becoming bogged down with a task. A quick check-in with a client to build rapport (a strength for you) can give you an energy boost before you return to the de-energising task. Another way to manage the de-energising quality of learned behaviours is to use them with other, more energising strengths.

Here's another example: You don't enjoy giving feedback but like boosting people's self-esteem. You can use strategies to provide feedback while also making them feel good. You could say, 'Hey Steve, I love how you courageously took action by calling that employer. Now, it's about following up with them. I wonder how good it would feel to follow up with them this week?'

It's important not to focus too much on your weaknesses. When you focus on improving or using your weaknesses, you are more likely to be parked in neutral or roll backward because you lose the drive to move forward. You are working from a place that is de-energising. When you focus on your strengths, you jump-start your life with energy you didn't know you had. You are more likely to move forward with the goals you want to achieve because you are working from a place of strength.

Once you have identified your strengths, nurture them! Invest in them! You will grow, develop, be more productive and love using them. As a job coach, this enhances your work experience and sets a powerful example for your clients. By embracing your strengths and values, you can light the way for others to do the same.

Strengths in action

When I started my company, Bounce, I was eager to help others find their way in work and life. But I hadn't fully understood and embraced my values and strengths. In one of my first Bounce Programs, I had a particularly challenging session with a participant who appeared extremely resistant to change. They were frustrated and reluctant to engage with me, and honestly, I felt a bit helpless.

After that challenging session, I took time to reflect. I asked myself the same questions I posed to my clients. What energises me? What motivates me? What excites me? What skills do I need to draw on to help me take a different approach?

In answering these questions, I realised that what I loved most was seeing people light up when they discovered something new about themselves. And with that moment of clarity, that spark of realisation, I was able to head back into the training room using my key strengths to engage with the participants.

Building rapport and creating safe spaces for open conversations are two key strengths of mine, and they would become the foundation of my interactions with program participants.

In my next session, instead of diving straight into problem-solving with the participant, I began with a simple yet powerful question: 'What makes you feel alive?' This shift in approach brought the conversation to life. They began sharing stories about their passions and dreams, and we gradually unpacked the values and strengths that mattered most to them.

This experience taught me the importance of playing to my strengths. It wasn't just about helping others. It was about aligning myself with what energised me to become a better coach. From that point on, I've made it a habit to integrate my strengths into my work, whether it was through energising conversations or creative problem-solving.

Reflecting on this now, I see how pivotal that moment was. It was a turning point that improved my coaching practice and brought a deeper sense of fulfilment to my professional life. By embracing my strengths, I found a way to connect more authentically with my clients and help them uncover their potential. And that, to me, is the true essence of being a job coach.

Practical Tool: Discover and celebrate your strengths

You might be curious now. What are my strengths? How do I easily identify them?

This activity will help you identify your realised and unrealised strengths, understand how to leverage them in your daily coaching practice and create a plan for nurturing and utilising them to achieve personal and professional goals.

1. Begin by reflecting on the concept of strengths. Think about times when you felt particularly energised and engaged in an activity. What were you doing? What made those moments special? Write down your thoughts.

2. Go to https://www.viacharacter.org/ and do the free survey, which is scientifically validated to help you discover your strengths. At Bounce, we use the Strengths Profile assessment, which is accredited by Strengths Profilers. https://bounceglobal.net/strength-profiling/

3. Now, reflect on ways to leverage your strengths to enhance your personal and professional life.

Write down some ways you can incorporate your strengths into your daily routine.

Strengths and values – a power couple

You make decisions aligned with what is important to you. Think about the goal you wanted from this program and the values that are met in achieving that goal. As a coach, I have clients who often find themselves in situations that are not aligned with their values, which can lead to low energy and increased negative emotions. Once they reflect on their values and start making decisions based on what is truly important to them, their values tend to change for the better.

The other core element of what makes us unique is our strengths. When we perform tasks that energise us and that we're good at, we can achieve incredible things. The secret here is doing more things that energise you and working them into all aspects of your life. If you feel energised by organising things, find a way to organise more in life or at work. If being connected to people energises you, consider joining groups or exploring other ways to meet people.

When you align your strengths and values, it increases your self-awareness and positive emotions. And ultimately, that's what we want more of.

'When we play to our strengths and our values are met, we become more satisfied.'

Actionable reflections

- Identify the core values that drive your decisions and assess how well your current actions align with them.

- Reflect on tasks that energise you and brainstorm ways to incorporate these into your daily professional and personal routines.

- Consider situations in life or work where your values are not being met and strategise ways to realign them.

- Explore opportunities to use your strengths in new ways, such as volunteering, networking or tackling projects aligned with your abilities.

- Set specific goals to align your values and

strengths, ensuring they contribute to long-term satisfaction and positive energy.

- Join groups, communities, or initiatives that resonate with your strengths and values to enhance your sense of connection and purpose.

- Evaluate past successes and identify how your strengths and values contributed to those achievements, using this insight to shape future decisions.

- Commit to regular self-reflection on how well you are leveraging your strengths and honouring your values in both professional and personal contexts.

Conclusion: Recognising what drives you

As you navigate your job coach journey, focus on your strengths and values to achieve your goals and success. By leveraging what makes you unique, you can overcome barriers, build confidence, and have a positive impact on your clients while enjoying your work. Embrace your values and strengths to thrive and create a ripple effect of positive change.

By embracing what makes you special, you can break down barriers and build confidence for yourself and your clients. Your work will become more than a job. It will become a mission infused with passion and authenticity. You'll find joy in both the small victories and the profound transformations.

Remember, the true essence of being a job coach lies in your ability to connect authentically, inspire courage, and empower those around you. Embrace your strengths and let them guide you to make a meaningful impact, both in your life and in the lives of those you touch. With this knowledge, we will head into the next chapter to learn how to protect your energy and emotions, allowing you to coach with confidence.

Chapter Three

The Three E's

Emotion, Energy and Empathy

Chris is an incredible job coach who pours her heart into her work. She is the kind of coach every client dreams of. She listens genuinely, goes above and beyond, and truly makes her clients feel seen and heard. I love catching up with her when I see her. Her energy is infectious, and her smile lights up the room.

When I first met her, she was new to the role and so excited to help every client achieve a positive employment outcome. She loved asking questions and was always completely engaged in conversations, listening with conscious awareness. Chris has a real skill for building rapport and connections with the people around her.

And I knew that her energy and empathy would serve her well, but only if she was able to protect it ...

Have you ever woken up brimming with excitement for the day ahead?

You feel energised, determined and ready to make a difference in your clients' lives. The kind of morning where you think, *'Today is going to be great!'* You head to work with a bounce in your step, but the first curveball hits: a colleague corners you to download their weekend drama, every minute in detail. You weren't there, but their blow-by-blow storytelling makes you feel like you were. Your enthusiasm takes a slight hit, but you shake it off. No big deal – I've got this.

Then, your first client doesn't show up. No problem, you think, shifting gears to tackle those unfinished case notes from the other day. But you can't help but notice your ten-out-of-ten energy slipping to an eight. Still, an eight is good. You push forward.

Your next client walks in carrying the weight of their world. Before you even have a chance to say much, they're venting, frustrated and distracted, barely present. You try to focus, but something shifts. Instead of thoroughly engaging, you retreat to the safety of the case notes, using them as a buffer. It feels like the spark you started the day with is dimming. A whisper of disappointment creeps in. Wasn't I feeling unstoppable an hour ago?

One by one, the appointments roll in. With each interaction, your energy dwindles. You become a little less present, a little more robotic – just checking boxes to get through the day. You skip your break. You have a back-to-back schedule with no room to pause, and by the time you wrap up your last session, your energy levels have slid down to a three or four.

Exhausted and drained, you walk out the door. Then it happens. A soft breeze, the sun warming your face, the crisp evening air filling your lungs. You feel a flicker of hope, a tiny dopamine boost. You think to yourself, tomorrow will be better. Tomorrow, I'll start again.

Maybe this resonates with you or feels like a distant thought, but I'm willing to bet you've had days like this. I know I have, and I teach this stuff! I've learned that sustaining your energy throughout the day isn't just a hope or a wish. It's a practice. It's about creating habits that fortify you to navigate the emotional demands of your work.

Your job is steeped in emotional labour. Every interaction demands your attention and energy. You're constantly drawing on empathy to connect, influence and inspire. You're the spark that activates hope in others, and that takes more than effort. It takes intention.

So, how do you keep that spark alive? How do you show up for your clients, your team and yourself with the energy that transforms moments and entire days? The answer lies in harnessing the power of the 3 E's and how these principles can elevate your coaching and fuel your energy, taking your day and impact to the next level.

Emotion: The secret catalyst for a fulfilling workday

Emotions are the invisible architects of our days, quietly shaping how we think, feel and act. They're not just fleeting states of mind; they're the driving force that can transform a routine workday into an inspiring journey. When you harness the power of positive emotions, you create a ripple effect that uplifts everyone around you, including your clients.

When working with unemployed clients, many of whom carry the weight of uncertainty, self-doubt and frustration, it's easy for their emotions to affect your energy. That's why positive emotions aren't just a *nice-to-have*. They are essential.

Positive emotions act as a shield and a bridge. They shield you from being pulled into the emotional turbulence of others and serve as a bridge to connect with clients on a deeper, more hopeful level. When you radiate positivity, you create a safe, motivating environment where clients can feel seen, heard and inspired to take steps toward change.

But how do you cultivate these positive emotions in a demanding role? It starts with small, intentional practices that prime your emotional energy. Imagine starting your day by writing three things you're grateful for, which becomes a powerful reminder of the good things in your life. Or perhaps take five minutes for mindfulness meditation, centring yourself before diving into the day. These simple acts act as emotional anchors, helping you remain grounded and resilient no matter what challenges come your way.

Now, think about what happens when you bring this positive energy to work with your clients. Your optimism becomes contagious. Instead of focusing on what's gone wrong, you help them see possibilities and opportunities. Your ability to maintain hope and enthusiasm encourages them to believe in themselves, even if they face rejection or setbacks. Positive emotions fuel empathy, creativity, and problem-solving, all of which are crucial when helping clients reimagine their futures. This might sound a little soft, fluffy or even 'woo-woo', but there's plenty of research-backed evidence that demonstrates the efficacy of positive emotions.

What does the science say?

Barbara Fredrickson, a renowned researcher in positive psychology, developed the Broaden-and-Build Theory[7], which reveals how positive emotions – such as joy, gratitude, and love – can profoundly influence our lives. These emotions expand our awareness, spark creativity, and encourage us to think and act in new, exploratory ways. Over time, this broadening effect helps us develop valuable resources, including physical strength, intellectual skills and social connections. For example, joy motivates play, interest fuels curiosity, and love drives us to connect deeply with others. These are the building blocks for resilience and adaptability, equipping us to better handle life's challenges.

Research indicates that positive emotions engage key brain regions, including the prefrontal cortex and hippocampus, and are crucial for decision-making, memory, and problem-solving. They stimulate the release of neurotransmitters like dopamine and serotonin, which are your brain's 'feel-good chemicals' that improve mood, motivation, and focus. Repeatedly experiencing these positive emotional states rewires your brain, strengthening neural pathways that make positivity and resilience your default.

> 'With positivity, you see new possibilities, bounce back from setbacks, connect with others, and become the best version of yourself.'
>
> Dr Barbara Fredrickson

So, how does this apply to your work? Maintaining your energy is crucial if you're in a high-emotional labour role, such as job coaching, where you need empathy to support your clients and positivity to spark hope in them. Simple, intentional habits like writing a gratitude list, practising mindfulness, or engaging in a quick, energising activity can give you the emotional boost you need. Practices like these are scientifically proven tools to enhance your wellbeing, interactions with clients and overall impact.

By prioritising positivity, you create a ripple effect. You show up for your clients with the energy and presence they need, inspiring them to take meaningful steps toward their goals. This may sound unconventional, but let me explain why it works for me and how it is transformative.

I start my day with a small but powerful practice every morning. A reminder on my phone pops up and simply says, 'Breathe. Get present.' It's my cue to pause, take a deep breath and connect with the moment.

From there, I focus on my intention for the day. I bring awareness to the things I need to stay aligned with, even when things get crazy busy or unexpected challenges pop up. That intention becomes the guide that helps me refocus if I feel overwhelmed or thrown off track.

For me, this isn't just a ritual – it's a superpower. And the best part? It's all within my control. I like to think of it as going to the gym, not for my body, but for my mind. Every time I do it, I strengthen my ability to stay present, positive and purposeful.

Cultivating positive emotions

Take a moment to think about how you feel at the start of your workday. What activities or practices help you feel energised and positive? Write down three strategies you can implement to boost your positive emotions each morning.

Here are a few ideas to get you started:

- Start your day with a gratitude journal. List three things you're thankful for to shift your mindset.

- Engage in quick physical activity, like brisk walking or stretching, to wake up your body and mind.

- Practice mindfulness or positive affirmations to ground yourself and set a clear, uplifting tone for the day.

The key is consistency. Making these practices part of your routine lays the groundwork for a successful and fulfilling day. You will boost your mood, build resilience and positively impact others. In a high-energy, emotionally demanding role, that's invaluable.

When you start your day by cultivating positivity, you set yourself up to show up fully for yourself and the people you support. Your energy and focus inspire hope and action in others. At the end of the day, you'll feel a deeper sense of purpose and fulfilment, knowing you stayed grounded and aligned with what matters most.

So, here's your challenge: take five minutes each morning to create your positive energy routine. Maybe it's a gratitude list, perhaps it's a short breathing practice, or maybe it's just setting a single intention for the day. Consider it a mental workout, like going to the gym, a step towards becoming a stronger, more resilient version of yourself.

Empathy is at the heart of coaching

Empathy is at the very core of what we do as job coaches. It allows us to connect with others deeply, understand their experiences, and provide meaningful support. But let's face it – while empathy is one of our greatest strengths, it can also feel overwhelming if we're not careful. Research by Paul Bloom highlights this challenge[8]. When empathy is stretched too far, it can lead to empathy fatigue and that drained, burnt-out feeling when we've cared so much for others that we forget to care for ourselves.

So, how do we keep empathy as our superpower while ensuring we don't burn out along the way?

Coach's insight: Chris's breakthrough

Three months into her role, Chris met John, a client who had been unemployed for over a year. John shared his struggles – the mounting financial pressure, the strain on his family relationships, and the countless rejections that left him feeling completely defeated. Chris listened intently, her heart breaking with every word. She felt John's pain as if it were her own.

Motivated to help, she dedicated hours to researching opportunities for John, crafting personalised job strategies, and even staying late to ensure he felt supported. But after a few weeks, something changed. Chris started to feel emotionally drained. She felt exhausted, lost focus and struggled to stay present for her other clients. Empathy fatigue had crept in. While her deep connection with John initially allowed her to provide exceptional support, it started taking a toll on her energy, enthusiasm and wellbeing.

I received an email from Chris not long after this. She was feeling really overwhelmed and asked me if I could help. Chris's breakthrough began not with doing more, but with a pause. I told her it was time to incorporate an 'empathy pause' into her coaching practice.

Encouraging her to name what she was feeling – depleted, stretched and emotionally full – in a quiet moment during the day would be helpful. This moment of honesty became the first step toward change. Rather than pushing through, she chose to step back, not from her clients, but from the belief that she must carry it all. She realised that supporting others doesn't have to mean sacrificing herself.

She began by adopting one simple habit: a five-minute empathy pause and breathing ritual between appointments. At first, it felt awkward, but soon, she noticed a shift. Her nervous system slowed. Her thoughts settled. Her presence sharpened. This became her anchor. Chris also started setting clear emotional boundaries at the end of each session using a short internal mantra, 'I was here, I cared, and now I let go.' These micro-practices allowed her to show up fully, without absorbing everything her clients brought into the room.

Many of us have experiences like Chris, especially in high-emotion roles like coaching. The key isn't to shut off empathy – it's about managing it to keep you energised and effective.

The *empathy pause* is a practice I swear by. At the end of each session, I take a moment to breathe, acknowledge the care I've shown, and mentally release any emotional weight that I don't need to carry forward. It's a small but powerful way to reset.

Another strategy is focusing on emotional resilience. For me, that might mean taking a quick walk between appointments, journaling at the end of the day, or scheduling intentional downtime. What works for you? It could be as simple as spending five minutes outside, practising gratitude, or listening to your favourite music.

If you're a Harry Potter fan, think of unchecked empathy fatigue as the effect of a Dementor. They are the scary creatures in cloaks covering their skeleton frames, floating around, feeding on happiness. Just as Dementors drain happiness and leave the person feeling hollow, taking on too much emotional weight can leave you depleted and unable to care as deeply as you'd like.

But here's the good news: you have your own Patronus Charm. Self-care, setting boundaries and focusing on positive emotions are your magical protection. Like Harry needed focus and happy memories to summon his Patronus, you need intentional habits to shield yourself from empathy fatigue.

Activity: The empathy reset

To help you harness empathy without burning out, here's a quick reflective practice:

Reflect on your boundaries: Write down one or two moments you felt drained after a session. What boundary could you have set to protect your energy?

Identify your recharge strategy: What helps you feel restored after a long day? Maybe it's a workout, calling a friend, or having some quiet time. Commit to doing this regularly.

Celebrate empathy wins: Take a moment to acknowledge the positive impact of your empathy on others. Reflect on a time when your support truly made a difference – it's a reminder of the power and purpose behind what you do.

Self-care plan: Develop a self-care plan that includes activities that rejuvenate and energise you. This could be exercise, meditation, hobbies or spending time with loved ones. Commit to incorporating these activities into your routine on a regular basis. I've developed an excellent self-care guide; if you'd like a free download, grab it here: https://bounceglobal.net/the-essential-guide-to-self-care/ .

Empathy in balance: Reflect on how to maintain empathy without overextending yourself. Consider practising 'rational compassion,' as suggested by Paul Bloom, which involves understanding and addressing others' needs without becoming emotionally overwhelmed[9].

Write down strategies you can implement to achieve this balance:

Balancing empathy through breathing

What's happening in your brain when you feel empathy? Mirror neurons are specialised brain cells that activate when we see someone else's emotions or actions. For instance, when you see a client smile, the same neurons fire in your brain as if you were smiling yourself. This creates a deep, almost automatic connection.

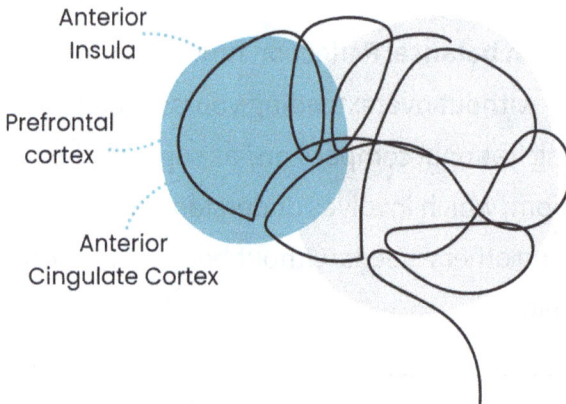

Anterior
Insula

Prefrontal
cortex

Anterior
Cingulate Cortex

Empathy & Your Brain

Empathy also engages the anterior insula (which processes emotions), the anterior cingulate cortex (which regulates emotions and helps us understand others' pain), and the prefrontal cortex (which enables us to take a perspective and make compassionate decisions). Here's the challenge: the same neural circuits that allow us to empathise can become overworked when constantly exposed to others' struggles. This triggers the brain's stress response, leaving us feeling emotionally exhausted.

Empathy is one of your greatest strengths, but like any strength, it needs care and attention. When you take the time to manage your empathy, you're protecting your wellbeing and ensuring you can continue showing up fully for your clients. Remember, self-care isn't selfish. It allows you to keep making a difference, one client at a time.

'Empathy is a choice, and it's a vulnerable one.'

Brené Brown

Practical Tool: Box Breathing Technique

So, how do we keep our empathy sustainable? The answer lies in activating the brain's relaxation system, the parasympathetic nervous system, through practices such as breathing, mindfulness, gratitude and self-compassion. These strategies are scientifically proven to help your brain reset and recharge. The simplest way to activate the parasympathetic nervous system is to down-regulate through breathing. I love box breathing because it can be done anywhere, anytime, and it works.

Box breathing is an effective way to manage stress and enhance wellbeing. Here's how you can practice it:

1. Start by sitting or standing and relaxing your body.

2. Breathe in for four counts.

3. Hold your breath for four counts.

4. Breathe out for four counts.

5. Hold for four counts.

6. Repeat until you feel calm and relaxed.

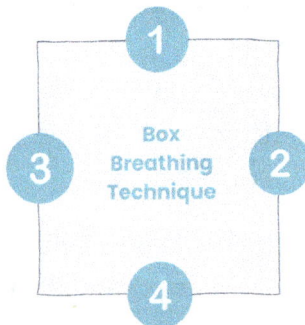

The Box Breathing Technique

This technique has been shown to relax the nervous system and calm the mind. It is particularly effective in high-stress situations and can be practised whenever you feel anxious about something you are about to do.

The benefits of box breathing include:

- Increased wellbeing

- Improved physical health

- Lowered blood pressure and heart rate

- Increased feelings of calm

Practice regularly: The more focused breathing you do, the easier it will be to create a good habit in your brain to call upon in times of stress.

Adapt to your needs: Not everyone needs to close their eyes while practising. Go at their own pace.

Empathy is your greatest strength as a coach, but it's also a tool that requires care and attention. Take the time to manage your empathy through small pauses, clear boundaries, or self-care to ensure that you keep showing up for your clients, day after day.

Relational energy: The hidden power in job coaching

Your energy level fuels your passion, drives your actions and influences the outcomes of your sessions. Imagine a day when you feel energised and motivated. Your enthusiasm is contagious and your clients can sense it. They become more engaged and willing to take risks, making them open to change. Relational energy is the powerful, positive energy exchanged between people through meaningful interactions. In Part 2, you'll learn how relational energy becomes an essential part of your coaching toolkit to activate hope with your clients.

Relational energy is the positive spark you get from a genuinely uplifting interaction. Imagine leaving a conversation feeling like you can conquer the world; that's the power of relational energy in action.

Scientific studies back up this magical feeling. Researchers have discovered that relational energy makes people feel more resourceful and emotionally charged (Owens & Patterson, 2013[10]; Baker, 2019[11]; Sumpter & Gibson, 2022[12]). During tough times, like a workplace crisis, this energy becomes a lifeline, increasing resilience and helping people navigate stress and uncertainty[13].

Now, picture this in the context of job coaching. A job coach with high relational energy infuses every session with positivity and encouragement, making you feel unstoppable. They transform a daunting job search into an exciting adventure, where every challenge is just a step towards a new opportunity. What's truly fascinating is how this energy transforms the relationship between the coach and the client. Relational energy can turn simple interactions and appointments into a life-changing partnership.

The relationship between a job coach and their client needs to move beyond transactional and become transformational. Yes, you're guiding someone through a critical life change, but it requires more than just knowledge of the labour market and the systems you use; it requires energy, trust, and a genuine human connection.

When I bring high relational energy to my coaching sessions, both my clients and I benefit. Positive, energising interactions make me feel more engaged and motivated in my work. The ripple effect of energy keeps me enthusiastic and driven, even in challenging times.

Trust is just as important to us as it is to our clients. When I feel a genuine connection with my clients, it deepens my sense of purpose and satisfaction in my role. This trust fuels my commitment and enthusiasm, making each session meaningful and impactful.

Building trust begins with being present, actively listening, and showing genuine interest in my clients' stories and aspirations. Creating a safe space where clients feel valued and understood is essential. Biswas-Diener and van Nieuwerburgh, in *Radical Listening: The Art of True Connection* (2024), describe how great communicators often take a moment to pause and centre themselves before engaging, reminding themselves that the conversation is not about them, but about fully focusing on the other person[14]. This intentional shift in presence is what allows us to put all of our listening onto the other person.

This space encourages open communication and deepens the connection. Being consistent also helps to reinforce trust. By being reliable and maintaining regular contact, even a quick check-in, your clients know you are holding time for them, demonstrating your commitment to their success. When your clients know they can rely on you, they are more likely to engage and trust you.

Relational energy and trust are intertwined. While I invest in building trust, the relational energy between my clients and me flourishes, creating a dynamic and productive coaching relationship.

Energy is contagious. I've noticed that it spreads to my clients when I'm in a positive state. This same principle applies to us as coaches. Cultivating high relational energy within myself means consistently bringing my best self to each session, benefiting my clients and enhancing my sense of fulfilment and success.

To be honest, working with some clients can be emotionally draining. Many job coaches face burnout due to job demands[15]. Think of relational energy like a battery. The more positive energy you put into your interactions, the more energised you feel in return. It's the difference between a coaching session that feels like pulling teeth and one that feels purposeful and uplifting.

So, how do I keep my relational energy high?

Here are some strategies that work for me:

Start with an energy check-in: Before each session, I ask myself, *'What energy am I bringing into this session? How do I want to feel afterwards?'*

Practice self-care: I make time for activities that recharge me, whether walking, breathing or stretching.

Reflect on positive interactions: After a particularly uplifting session, I take a moment to reflect on what made it so energising and how I can replicate that in future interactions.

When I bring high relational energy to my work, I help my clients succeed, and I remain enthusiastic, motivated, and fulfilled.

This personal approach to maintaining high relational energy has transformed my coaching practice, making every session an opportunity for both my clients and me to thrive. It's a win-win!

Activity: Cultivating relational energy

How do you use relational energy in your day-to-day work? Here are practical ways to bring more energy into your coaching sessions and help your clients achieve their best.

Begin with an energy check-in before meeting a client.

Ask yourself:

- *What energy am I bringing into this session?*

- *How do I want my client to feel after this interaction?*

- *What's one small thing I can do to set the right tone?*

Simple actions like smiling, making eye contact and showing genuine enthusiasm can shift the entire dynamic.

Practical Tool: The Energy Grid

The Energy Grid is a tool to help you quickly and easily identify what energises you and what drains your energy levels.

Complete the table below:

1. **Identify Energy Sources:** List activities, thoughts or habits that energise you before coaching sessions.

2. **Pinpoint Energy Drainers:** What diminishes your energy? Avoid these before client

interactions.

3. **Set Relational Energy Goals:** Write down three ways you will project positive energy in your next session.

Energy Sources	Energy Drainers

Relational Energy Goals
1.
2.
3.

Your relational energy goals might include:

- Start with a warm greeting and a smile.

- Share one success story relevant to your client.

- Conclude with a motivating takeaway or next step.

Your relational energy is one of the most powerful tools at your disposal as a job coach. It turns an everyday conversation into a life-changing moment for your clients.

So, the next time you sit down with a client, ask yourself:

- *Am I bringing the energy that will inspire action?*

- *How can I use relational energy to create a shift for this person?*

Because when you show up with belief, energy and optimism, your clients will also start to believe in themselves. And that's when everything changes.

Actionable reflections

- Bring intentional energy into every coaching session to inspire action and transformation in your clients.

- Use relational energy as a tool to create meaningful shifts and breakthroughs in conversations.

- Reframe expectations before a session and approach each interaction with belief and optimism to set a positive tone.

- Recognise the contagious nature of your energy. When you bring hope and belief, your clients will mirror those emotions.

- Establish boundaries to prevent empathy fatigue and maintain your effectiveness as a coach.

- Replenish your emotional reserves regularly to sustain your ability to uplift and guide others.

Remember that coaching is about your way of being, not just the advice or strategies you provide.

Conclusion: Show up fully without burning out

Emotion, empathy and energy are the invisible forces shaping coaching success. Without them, even the best advice won't resonate. Every session begins with the energy you bring, whether it's bracing for resistance or fostering belief and hope.

Your energy is contagious. When you show up with belief and optimism, your clients mirror that, unlocking potential for transformation and breakthrough. Empathy without exhaustion is key. Too much can lead to fatigue, draining your ability to uplift others. Protecting your energy isn't selfish – it ensures you're present and effective. When you align your emotions, empathy and energy, you become the difference, activating hope within your clients that they can achieve success.

Shifting Gears ...

Now, it's time to shift gears. Part 1 laid the foundation for personal transformation. In Part 2, we will apply that solid groundwork to helping others, especially those who are the most difficult to reach.

Part 2

Activating Hope in Your Clients

Moving from insight to impact

Welcome to the next stage of our journey together. If you're here, it means you're ready to dive deeper and make an even greater impact on the lives of those you coach.

In Part 1, we focused on you, the coach. We explored how self-awareness, strengths, values and relational energy influence your presence at work. You reflected on your beliefs, examined how you connect with people, and learnt how to bring your best self into every coaching conversation.

Coaching conversations are where the magic happens, and we move from insight to impact. Job Coaches need to think beyond just understanding people and see themselves as igniters of hope! Why? Hope is the catalyst that turns insight into action, resilience and the courage to keep moving forward.

When I was working on my Master's degree in Applied Positive Psychology, I knew I wanted my capstone project to be something more than just an academic endeavour. It had to be helpful, practical and genuinely impactful, capable of making a lasting difference in people's lives. So, I focused it on something close to my heart – activating hope in people who've been out of work for a long time.

I began with a simple yet powerful question: What if we could intentionally *cultivate hope in someone who had lost it completely?* What if hope wasn't something you had or didn't have, but something we could help people feel again?

Drawing from Charles Snyder's Hope Theory[16], where hope is described as having clear goals, the motivation to pursue them, and the ability to figure out how to get there, I began to imagine a new way job coaches could work with people.

Through my research, I found that hope can be *activated* in people. Not through big, sweeping changes or grand motivational speeches, but through genuine connection, relational energy and consistent, supportive human interactions. The kind of conversations where someone feels seen. Where someone dares to believe that maybe, just maybe, something new is possible for them.

The people we work with often face more than just unemployment. They may feel isolated, ashamed or mentally exhausted, and the psychological work-readiness skills we want to see, like confidence, motivation and resilience, can feel like distant memories. And when the system becomes too focused on ticking boxes and chasing outcomes, people fall through the cracks, and so do the job coaches trying to help them.

That's what inspired me to create the **Hope Activation Model**.

I wanted to develop a structured, practical approach for job coaches that went beyond compliance and into connection. The Model is a way to transform everyday interactions into hope-inspiring, future-shaping conversations. When we help someone feel hopeful again, we're not just helping them find work; we're helping them believe in their future.

The Hope Activation Model is built on the idea that hope is not a fixed trait, but a state that can be nurtured, supported, and grown, especially when someone struggles to see the light for themselves.

You might wonder, *'How do I activate hope in someone who has lost faith in themselves?'* Building the skill of social awareness enables you to read the room, sense what's unspoken, and respond in ways that build trust and connection. But social awareness alone isn't enough. We need to go beyond it. We must inspire, uplift and show others that change is possible and within their reach.

Through the Hope Activation Model, the role of the job coach becomes crucial. The goal is to transition from a purely transactional relationship to one that is deeply relational and supportive.

Seeing and hearing the client: The first step is to make clients feel genuinely seen and heard. This means actively listening to their stories, struggles and aspirations without judgment.

Providing relational energy: The job coach must bring energy and optimism into the relationship. This positive relational energy can spark change and inspire clients to believe in their potential.

Focusing on holistic growth: Instead of solely concentrating on job placement, the focus includes building the client's confidence, resilience and self-belief. This approach prepares clients for both job opportunities and other aspects of life.

By following these principles, job coaches can help clients move from a place of hopelessness to one of empowerment, where they see real possibilities for their future.

Explaining the Hope Activation Model

This model visually represents how hope is activated and sustained through the dynamic relationship between the client and the job coach. It's based on Snyder's Hope Theory, which says that hope requires two key elements:

- **Will:** The internal motivation or belief that change is possible.

- **Way:** The ability to see a path forward or create a plan to achieve a goal.

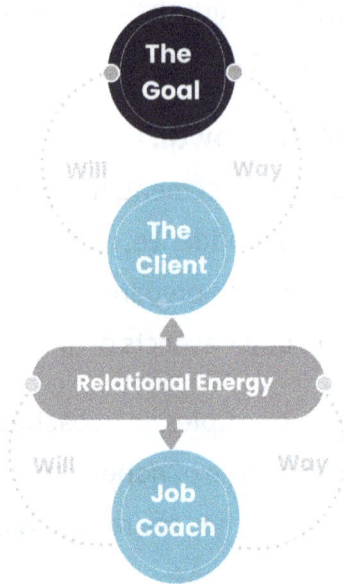

The Hope Activation Model

In this model:

- At the top, we see the goal, something the client wants to achieve. This might be employment, confidence, housing, independence, or a sense of purpose.

- The client sits in the middle, surrounded by the concepts of will and way.

- But here's the magic: relational energy flows between the job coach and the client.

That energy exchange is what activates hope. The supportive, intentional, human connection helps the client build the will to move forward and believe they can find a way.

In turn, the job coach must also hold a sense of 'will and way', meaning they must stay hopeful, creative and resilient. The model reminds us that the coach's mindset and energy aren't just background factors but are essential in activating hope for someone else.

Part 2 of this book focuses on utilising the model to inspire hope in others. As a job coach, I encourage you to think beyond words and ideas to truly make a lasting impact on people's lives. By developing deep social awareness, practising empathy and fostering genuine connections, we can help people believe in themselves again.

So, let's embark on this next chapter with enthusiasm and determination. Together, we can transform disengagement into engagement, despair into hope and inaction into purposeful action.

The key to activating hope? Deep social awareness combined with intentional action.

Chapter Four

Social Awareness

The Beginning of Hope

*The early days of the Bounce Program™ (almost 20 years ago!) I found myself working with a lot of participants who were enrolled in the program because they **had** to, not because they wanted to.*

I recall a participant named Sam, who looked me directly in the eye and casually announced, 'I don't want to work.' They said it without apology, without anger, just as a matter of fact. The statement, which matched their body language, was so unemotional, it took me by surprise. I jumped straight into solution mode and did what many well-meaning coaches do, thinking of all the reasons why Sam could feel this way. Maybe it's a confidence issue, I thought. Perhaps if we build their self-belief, they'll start to see work as a possibility.

I started planning questions, lining them up like stepping stones in my head. Without hesitating, I started asking questions, expecting insightful answers to help guide our direction. What is something you've done before that made you feel capable? Who's someone in your life who believed in you? What would confidence look like for you?

But as I launched into the questions, I noticed a shift. Sam leaned back, arms folded and dropped their head. They appeared completely closed off, shut down and disengaged from me. And I remember thinking, 'Huh? That's odd. What just happened?'

It wasn't until much later, when I reflected on that session, that it hit me. I hadn't really been present with Sam. Sure, I was listening, but I wasn't present. I was so caught up trying to be helpful and asking the right questions that I'd missed what was right in front of me. I didn't stay in their world. I didn't tune into their emotional space. I was aware of them, but I wasn't attuned to them …

If you've ever sat across from a disengaged client, arms crossed, eyes low, offering little more than a shrug, you'll know that sinking feeling. It's frustrating. You might wonder, *'Why won't they meet me halfway?'*

But here's the thing – disengagement is rarely about you. For your clients, there will be things happening below the surface that will impact their behaviour, motivation and engagement. Over time, layers of rejection, fear, shame or survival have accumulated. For many of the people we work with, unemployment is only one of the loads they are carrying. They've experienced years of being overlooked, knocked back and made to feel like they don't matter.

What you're seeing isn't resistance, it's more often a complete loss of hope. And this is where your real work as a job coach begins.

Your role isn't simply to help someone land a job or career. You can help your clients see that they have something to offer, that change is possible and that they are not stuck. In fact, you can help them see that another future is waiting for them.

The first step in that journey? Social awareness.

Social awareness is your ability to read the room, tune into what's unspoken and respond in a way that builds trust, safety and connection. But awareness alone isn't enough. To help someone move forward, we must also activate hope, because hope fuels motivation, resilience and the courage to try again.

That moment I had with Sam in the Bounce Program taught me something I carry with me every day as a coach. Being an effective coach is not just about asking the right questions. Coaches need to pay deep, respectful attention to the person sitting in front of us.

When someone says, *'I don't want to work,'* they aren't lazy or apathetic. They are more likely to feel fear, shame or hopelessness, and unless we tune in and listen beneath the words, we'll miss the chance to deeply connect.

That one session changed how I show up. Now, I pause more and let silence exist. I breathe. I notice. Because being fully present isn't just a nice-to-have, it's everything.

Developing social awareness

Think of social awareness as being a quiet detective of emotion. You want to notice the cues others don't say out loud. Having social awareness is your ability to:

- read body language and tone

- notice shifts in energy or mood

- pick up on the fears, frustration or doubt floating silently in the space between words.

Imagine sitting in a theatre. The actors deliver their lines flawlessly, but the story is more than just what you see on the screen. It's in the *pauses*, the *glances*, the *subtle shifts in posture*. That's social awareness. You can sense what's happening between the lines and respond with empathy instead of assumption.

Social awareness doesn't mean you have to be overly intuitive or *great with people*. You can be socially aware by being fully present, tuning in emotionally to the shared space you're in with someone and adjusting how you show up in response.

Daniel Goleman, a leading expert on emotional intelligence, defines social awareness as:

'The ability to understand other people's emotions, needs, and concerns, pick up on emotional cues, feel comfortable socially, and recognise the power dynamics in a group or organisation.' [17]

In practice, it's not grand or dramatic. It often shows up in subtle moments like:

- a pause before someone talks about a past failure

- a flicker in their voice when they say, *'I don't care anymore.'*

- tension on their shoulders when you mention interviews

- that tight smile that doesn't quite reach their eyes.

These are the moments where your awareness becomes a powerful tool for connection.

Social awareness goes beyond the words someone says and encourages you to pay attention to what the person is not saying. Recognising the internal battles playing out behind the mask of *'I'm fine'* is crucial. Interpreting what someone's body, face, or silence might be telling you is an essential skill.

Picture a client who says, *'I'm fine with whatever happens,'* but you notice a small tremor in their hands. That one detail might reveal a deeper anxiety or fear. And that moment, when you see without judgment, is where trust begins. You don't need to fix it. You just need to be fully present. Your presence alone can say, *'You're safe here. I see you. You matter.'*

I can't tell you how often I've sat with a client and intentionally focused all my attention on them, which I frequently refer to as being fully present, *with all my looking and all my listening.*

Even when someone says, *'Yes, I'm going to do that,'* I don't just take the words at face value. I tune in to their body language, tone and energy. I'm watching for those subtle cues that tell me whether their words and their truth are aligned. Because often, what's not said is where the real story lives.

This kind of presence, truly seeing someone, not just hearing them, creates the space for more profound insight. It helps us gently unpack what might be holding them back from taking that next step. We become clearer guides when we listen beyond words and offer safety through our presence. Not because we have the answers, but because we're paying attention to the whole human in front of us.

When someone feels truly seen, without being pushed, judged or rushed, they soften. They begin to let you in. And sometimes, that's the first moment they've done that in a long time. That's the beginning of hope.

When you develop social awareness, you stop coaching from a script and start coaching from a place of deep presence and care. You become:

- a mirror, gently reflecting what's really going on

- a guide, helping people find clarity and confidence

- a safe space where clients can finally be honest without fear.

You're not just helping someone get a job. You're helping them discover their potential and possibilities.

Coach's insight: Sam's breakthrough

On day four of the Bounce Program™, I took a different approach with Sam. I'd lost some trust and rapport with them after my direct line of questions, and I knew I needed to reconnect with more awareness and authenticity.

During a solo activity that involved creating a vision board, I noticed Sam carefully cutting out pictures of biscuits from magazines and catalogues and placing them on the cardboard. Approaching with quiet curiosity, I commented, 'That's looking amazing, Sam. What an interesting collection of pictures you've found.' Sam met my gaze slowly with gentle eyes, an ever-so-slight smile creeping onto their face. I matched her small smile and carefully lowered myself to the floor so I wasn't standing over them at the table.

'I'm curious about why you picked these images for your vision board. Can you tell what they mean to you?'

In that moment, Sam's shoulders softened, and they let out a slow breath. 'When I was little, my nan used to make biscuits all the time for me. My mum wasn't around much, so I spent a lot of time with her after school and on weekends. She was a great cook!'

In that moment, I knew I'd found a new connection with Sam. We chatted about flavours and textures for quite a while, and I noticed that with each minute, Sam warmed up to me even more. Matching her energy, I was able to start asking more questions and getting more information from Sam that could help in their journey to finding a job.

By the end of the program, Sam had opened up to others in the training room and on the last day, they even brought in a tray of homemade biscuits to share. They'd decided to explore options for further training in hospitality and were even considering a side hustle in biscuit baking. Sam was feeling more hopeful about their pathway forward, and the energy shift was remarkable.

Social awareness, empathy, and relational energy – The heart of Hope Activation

Human-to-human connection sits at the centre of the Hope Activation Model, and the driving force is relational energy. In Chapter 3, we discussed the power of emotions, empathy and relational energy, and now you'll see how they feed into the Hope Activation Model.

In this model, hope is made up of two essential elements:

- **Will:** The motivation and belief that change is possible.

- **Way:** The ability to see pathways toward change.

These components live in both the client and the job coach, and relational energy is what links them together.

As a coach, your job is to help your client strengthen their will and find their way. But here's something we don't talk about enough – you need your own **will** and **way,** too.

Let's break it down ...

Coach's Will: Your belief in the client's possibility

Your will is your inner resolve to stay patient, present, and committed, even when your clients don't believe in themselves. Your will fuels you to keep showing up with empathy instead of frustration and curiosity instead of judgment.

For example:

A client says, *'No one's going to hire me anyway.'*

Your will says: *'I believe something else is possible for you. And I'm not going anywhere.'*

You hold hope for them until they can hold it for themselves.

Coach's Way: Your strategies and tools

This is where your coaching practice comes in and your questioning skills, frameworks and ability to shift conversations from stuck to forward-moving.

For example:

You might gently reframe a moment of resistance with, *'I get why you'd feel that way, and let's explore the things that have worked for you. Maybe there's something we can learn to help us find a new way forward.'*

That's you using your way, your skillset, to open a door they thought was locked.

> *'Hope is the sum of the mental willpower and waypower that you have for your goals.'*
> Charles Snyder

When your will and way align with your client, and when you're socially aware enough to notice where they are emotionally, relational energy begins to build. We discussed relational energy in Chapter 3, and how to protect and maintain energy with your clients. We want you to bring this positive energy into your sessions to activate hope with your clients.

Relational Energy is not something you can fake or force. It emerges when:

- you're fully present

- you respond to their cues with compassion

- you adjust your approach based on what they need, not what the system expects.

In that space, trust grows. And in that trust, hope is activated.

Hope in action

Let's say a client shows up late and disengaged. They give short answers and avoid eye contact. If you only think about outcomes, you might rush to ask about job goals or resume updates. However, if you're socially aware, you'll notice the cues, including a flat tone, low energy and closed body language. You'll shift gears.

You might say:

'Thanks for being here. I sense you've got some things going on? Would it help to talk about where you're at today before we get into the next steps?'

That moment? That's relational energy in motion.

Using your **will** (patience and presence) and your **way** (empathic communication) will help you reconnect and re-engage. You're not just delivering a service; you're activating a sense of possibility.

In the Hope Activation Model, progress doesn't come from ticking boxes. It comes from a deep connection and moments when someone feels truly seen and supported. Your social awareness fuels your empathy, and empathy in turn fuels relational energy. Relational energy unlocks the will and way that sparks lasting change.

Remember, my Bounce Program™ participant Sam? After just two weeks in the training room, they went from being uninterested in working to exploring further training options. With some time and focus on finding the will and the way, Sam was able to feel hopeful about their future.

How to develop social awareness and activate hope

These five steps can help you develop your social awareness and activate hope in your clients.

1. Read what's not being said

Your client may not immediately express that they feel hopeless. Instead, they might:

- Shrug and say, *'I don't care about getting a job.'*

- Avoid eye contact and give one-word answers.

- Show up late or miss appointments.

Instead of reacting with frustration, try to remain curious. Ask:

- *'Tell me more about that.'*

- *'If I could wave a magic wand and change one thing for you, what would it be?'*

- *'What's something that used to make you excited?'*

Hope isn't activated by forcing someone to care but by helping them feel seen.

2. Validate before you motivate

When people are feeling hopeless, motivation alone won't be enough to pull them out. If a client says, *'There's no point in applying for jobs. No one ever hires me.'*, telling them, *'You just need to be positive!'* won't help.

Your response: Acknowledge first, then reframe.

- *'I hear you. It makes sense that you'd feel that way after everything you've been through.'* **(validation)**

- *'Can I share something I've seen? I've worked with people who felt the same way, and things changed when we took a different approach.'* **(hope activation)**

When people feel understood, they become more open to possibility.

3. Use silence to create space

Job coaches often feel pressured to fill every gap with advice or encouragement. But silence is where breakthroughs happen.

Instead of immediately jumping in with solutions, try:

- Noticing when a client hesitates before answering.

- Pausing instead of rushing to the next question.

- Letting them sit in their own thoughts.

Clients need space to process and take ownership of hope.

4. Shift the focus from jobs to strengths

The employment-first approach often backfires because clients feel pressured to jump into work, which they're not emotionally ready for.

Instead of asking, *'What job do you want?'*, start with:

- *'What's something you're naturally good at?'*

- *'Tell me about a time you felt proud of something you did.'*

- *'What kind of work makes you feel comfortable and confident?'*

The aim is to activate self-efficacy and a belief in their ability to succeed. Your clients need to activate agency, meaning they believe they can do something, because they've previously experienced success. This is their **will**.

5. Model hope in the way you show up

Clients pick up on your energy. If you're going through the motions, they will, too. But if you show up with warmth, enthusiasm and belief in their potential, even when they don't see it themselves, you plant the first seed of hope.

Practical ways to model hope:

- Use encouraging body language (lean in, smile, nod).

- Speak positively *'I know you can do this.'*

- Celebrate small wins, not just job outcomes *'That was a great conversation. You handled it really well!'*

The goal isn't just to find a job but to help them believe they can do more.

Practical Tool: The Hope Map

When working through this process with your clients, you can use a simple tool called The Hope Map. It's a visual tool to help your clients reflect on the resources and strategies they need to help them achieve their goals.

You can access The Hope Map here: https://bounceglobal.net/the-hope-map/.

Activity: Hope activation journal

This exercise is designed to help you bring the Hope Activation Model to life in your coaching practice. It's simple, reflective and powerful. You'll explore how to reignite hope in your clients by examining your own approach and energy.

Choose a client – someone you've worked with recently who seemed stuck, defeated or disconnected. Think about the interaction carefully and use the prompts below to guide your reflection.

1. Observe Without Judgement

- What did you notice about their body language, tone, or energy?

- What might have been happening beneath the surface that they didn't say out loud?

2. Your Own Beliefs

- What beliefs did you hold about this client's potential?

- Were there moments where doubt crept in? How did you keep your vision for their success alive?

3. Your Coaching Approach

- What questions or strategies did you use to help them open up?

- How did you steer the conversation toward progress? (Our next chapter will dive deeper into the power of questions)

4. The Energy Exchange

- How did you show up in that moment? (Consider your body language, tone or overall energy.)

- How did their energy shift in response to yours?

5. Sparking Hope

- Was there even the tiniest moment where hope flickered in the session?

- What did you do or not do that made space for

that glimmer of hope?

Now, take a moment to reflect. How can you bring even more intention and focus to activating hope in your next conversation? Write down your thoughts, and don't be afraid to dig deep. This small act of reflection could transform how you show up for your clients and how they show up for themselves.

Grab your journal, take 15 minutes and work through these prompts. You'll be amazed at how much clarity and insight you can uncover. Not only will this help you grow as a coach, but it will also ignite a spark in your clients that could change their lives.

Actionable Reflections

- Hope can be reignited – even when it feels lost. Consistent coaching conversations can spark hope in people who have stopped believing in themselves.

- Social awareness is where hope begins. By noticing body language, silence, and emotional cues, you build trust for clients to open up.

- You are the holder of hope. Clients often need

someone to see them and believe in them until they can believe again.

- Relational energy is the bridge. The Hope Activation Model connects the client's *will* and *way* to action through the coach-client energy.

- Your presence matters more than your answers. Deep listening and empathy are your most powerful tools in each session.

- Reflect on your journey. Remember how far you've come and use those experiences to fuel your coaching sessions. Your story can inspire others to find their way back to hope.

Conclusion: Be guided by a little bit of hope

Hope is where change begins, but it's not where it ends. What you've just explored is the heart of transformational coaching. Being the one who sees possibility when your client cannot, who listens beyond the words, and who brings presence when all they've known is pressure.

By activating hope, you've laid the emotional groundwork. You've helped someone remember who they are, what they're capable of, and that they are not alone in this journey. But hope needs fuel, and that fuel is motivation.

What prompts someone to take that initial step? What shifts them from knowing they can to believing they will?

In our next chapter, we'll unpack the psychological drivers behind human behaviour. You'll learn why some clients stay stuck and what unlocks their desire to move. We'll dive into Self-Determination Theory, explore autonomy, competence and connection, and show you how to reframe resistance, ask catalytic questions and support lasting change.

Chapter Five

Motivation and Change

Why People Do and Don't Take Action

*'Human beings have an innate inner drive
to be autonomous, self-determined, and
connected to one another.'*

Daniel Pink

Firstly, well done on making it this far on your journey
to becoming an outstanding job coach. How are you
feeling right now? Has the experience been one of twists
and turns? Or are you feeling like your pathway is clear,
guiding you straight ahead?

So far, you've deepened your self-awareness, explored how to activate hope in your clients, and learned the importance of social awareness. Now, we turn to something essential in the coaching – understanding what truly motivates people and why change can feel so hard.

Whether you're helping someone return to work, explore a new opportunity, or simply stay engaged, it all hinges on one question: *What makes people move?*

Have you ever been really excited about an idea, like a fire lighting up inside you and whispering, *'Yes, this is it!'*?

Maybe it was deciding to try a new recipe, starting a small garden, signing up for a class, or finally asking a friend to hang out. You felt that spark, remembered it and told yourself, *'I'm going to do this.'* And then ... you didn't.

There's no shame here. I've been there too! More times than I care to admit. For years, I thought there was something wrong with me. I was a high achiever, deeply committed to personal growth, and yet, I'd let little dreams slip away.

One that sticks with me was when I decided to run a half-marathon. It felt like the perfect challenge, something to push me physically and mentally. I imagined crossing that finish line with the wind in my hair, arms raised in triumph. I was committed. I started strong, mapped out my training plan, laced up my shoes, and even began sharing my intention with others. I felt the buzz.

But then life happened.

I missed a training day. Then another. *'It's okay,'* I told myself, *'I'll go tomorrow.'* But tomorrow came and went. My goal slowly turned from a burning desire into a lukewarm idea. Eventually, it became something I talked about doing, not something I was actually doing.

I was frustrated. How could I, someone who teaches motivation and behaviour change for a living, not motivate myself? That question sent me into a deep dive, not just into my own patterns, but into the psychology behind why we do, or don't, take action.

Here's what I discovered: I hadn't really owned that goal.

On the surface, it looked like a great idea. But if I'm honest, the motivation wasn't coming from deep within me. It was driven by external reasons, such as wanting to look fit, be part of something impressive, and ticking off another achievement on my goals list. There wasn't enough intrinsic fuel in the tank. And when the weather got cold or my calendar got full, that borrowed motivation ran dry.

That's when Self-Determination Theory lit up my brain like a flare in the night. Unlocking the power of motivation often feels like navigating a winding road. The research that underpins the concepts of motivation is essential for you to explore and understand, so you can see how the different systems in our brain interact and open doors to coaching that truly empowers individuals.

Self-Determination Theory (SDT)[18] teaches us that, just like a well-tuned vehicle, autonomy, competence and relatedness are the gears that drive meaningful change. But what happens when the road becomes foggy, and the brain's emotional autopilot – System 1 – takes the wheel?

In this chapter, we'll explore the forces that drive and sometimes stall human action. You'll discover practical tools and fresh perspectives to better understand motivation, navigate the complexities of change, and help your clients find their spark when the road ahead feels uncertain.

Fuel for the journey

Let's imagine for a moment that your client is a little Kombi van – quirky, capable and full of potential. Strange metaphor, I know, but stay with me!

Your client has got a destination in mind, maybe even a dream they haven't quite said out loud yet. But their engine's idling. Maybe they're unsure of the road ahead. Perhaps they've stalled at the first red light. Maybe they don't even believe the road is meant for them.

As a coach, you're not the mechanic. You're the map-holder, the navigator, sometimes even the roadside cheerleader. This chapter is about understanding what gets that van rolling again.

When I first began working in this space, I was fascinated (and at times, frustrated) by why some people took off with gusto while others seemed stuck. I could see smart, capable people who just couldn't seem to move forward. That curiosity led me deep into the psychology of motivation and change, where I discovered a whole new world that transformed my coaching approach.

You don't need to fix your clients. You just need to understand the psychology that powers them and how to ask the right questions at the right time.

Let's fill the tank, check the mirrors and hit the road.

According to researchers Deci and Ryan[19], for any of us to sustain motivation, three basic needs must be met:

- **Competence**: I need to feel like I can do it.

- **Autonomy**: I need to feel like I chose it.

- **Relatedness**: I need to feel connected to others in the process.

Looking back, I lacked autonomy. It was a *should*, not a *want*. I wasn't feeling competent. Each missed training day chipped away at my confidence. And I didn't bring anyone else along for the ride, so I lacked the connection and support that would've helped carry me through.

The other key lightbulb moment stemmed from Nobel Prize-winning researcher and psychologist Daniel Kahneman's concept of System 1 and System 2 thinking[20]. I was relying too heavily on willpower. I wasn't tapping into System 2's slow, deliberate thinking, and most often letting System 1 hijack the steering wheel. It was easier, more familiar and more comfortable to skip the run and stay home. My brain defaulted to the path of least resistance.

Now, when I work with clients who struggle to take action, even when they say they want something, I understand their struggles. I've been there. And I know it's not about laziness or lack of discipline. It's about alignment.

If I didn't act on something I truly cared about, imagine how tough it is for someone facing unemployment, rejection and self-doubt. Your clients aren't broken, they're human. Like all of us, they need more than a good idea to take action. They need the right fuel, the right spark and the right support.

The Psychology of Motivation: Self-Determination Theory

Self-Determination Theory (SDT)[21] helps us understand human motivation from the inside out. According to SDT, people are naturally inclined toward growth, development, and change if the three basic psychological needs are met:

1. Competence – 'I can do this.'

People are more likely to act when they feel capable. If your client believes they lack the necessary skills or knowledge to succeed, they will likely be hesitant to take the first step. As a coach, build up their sense of mastery by identifying their strengths, reinforcing progress and helping them build one skill at a time.

Coach Prompt: *'What's something you already know how to do that could help here?'*

2. Autonomy – 'I choose to do this.'

When people feel like they have choice and control, they're more motivated to act. This is why collaborative goal-setting and client-led problem-solving are essential. Let them lead, while you guide the way.

Coach Prompt: *'What would feel like the next right move for you?'*

3. Relatedness – 'I belong here.'

Connection matters. People are more likely to act when they feel supported and seen. Creating a safe, trusting space in your coaching relationship is not just good practice; it's motivational fuel.

Coach Prompt: *'Who can you share this goal with to feel more connected and supported?'*

Your clients may experience all of these in their lives. The feeling of being alone and disconnected, especially in a system that can be more transactional. Or feeling like they do not have autonomy or control over the system they have to navigate, such as attending appointments or fulfilling their Centrelink obligations, which decreases their sense of control over their life. Finally, their sense of competency is directly impacted by not working and developing skills. Recent Australian research by Dr Cheryl Sykes (2023) supports this finding. Her study found that job seekers in the *JobActive* system often felt isolated and unsupported, with the three basic needs consistently undermined, which reduced motivation and negatively impacted their wellbeing[22].

> '*The highest-quality motivation is self-determined or autonomous.*'
>
> Edward Deci

Coach's insight: Ryan's breakthrough

I once had a young guy named Ryan in a Bounce Program™. From the moment he walked in, it was clear he wasn't exactly thrilled to be there. He told me straight up he didn't want a job. He wasn't lazy or disengaged; he was just uninterested. He didn't see the point of working for someone else when he was already making money selling stuff online. He was only at Bounce because he had to be there to meet his Centrelink requirements.

The old me might have gone into solution mode and tried to convince him of the value of employment, its structure, the income and the long-term benefits. But this wasn't about convincing. It was about connecting.

Instead, I got curious. I asked him to tell me more about what he was doing online. As he discussed his small business, including finding stock and managing sales, I noticed his whole demeanour shift. He lit up. This wasn't just a hustle to get by. This was something he cared about.

That was the spark. And that's where Self-Determination Theory came alive in real-time.

Autonomy – 'I choose this.'

Ryan wasn't motivated by external pressure. He wanted freedom. The idea of going into a 9-to-5 job didn't inspire him, but building his own business? That was his choice. I didn't push him into employment. I reflected on what I had seen. 'You've already started a business, Ryan. What if you could grow it and never need to rely on benefits again?' He paused. That landed.

I introduced him to the New Enterprise Incentive Scheme (NEIS), now known as the Self-Employment Assistance (SEA) program. It offered business mentoring, training and financial support. Suddenly, what felt like another 'requirement' for him suddenly became a launchpad for his own vision.

Competence – 'I can do this.'

At first, Ryan wasn't sure he could run a 'real' business. Selling online felt casual, something he fell into, not something he could scale. So, we worked on his skills. Through participating in the NEIS program, he developed a comprehensive business plan, gained a basic understanding of financials, and refined his customer approach. Every step built his confidence. Each small win, from obtaining his ABN to setting up his branding and securing his first repeat customers, became a marker of mastery.

Relatedness – 'I belong here.'

In the Bounce room, he went from a disinterested participant to a contributor. Other participants started asking him for advice. He offered tips on pricing, online tools and where to find stock. That sense of being seen, not as someone avoiding work, but as someone resourceful and innovative, changed everything. He wasn't a 'difficult' client anymore. He was an entrepreneur in the making.

Ryan applied for the NEIS program and was accepted. He transitioned from welfare to running his business full-time. He later messaged me to say that it was the first time he felt like someone had listened, not tried to change him, but helped him channel his energy toward something that felt right for him.

Motivation isn't about pushing someone into a box. It's about unlocking what already matters to them and aligning that with opportunities that build competence, foster autonomy and create connection. Ryan didn't need fixing. He needed someone to reflect his potential back to him and help remove the barriers between where he was and where he could go. That is the power of SDT. And that's the power of coaching with curiosity, not control.

System 1 & System 2: How the brain drives (and derails) change

When clients resist change, it's rarely because they don't want to grow. Instead, old patterns often override their values, needs or emotions. Usually, what's hidden beneath resistance is a misalignment with their deeper motivations, something we'll explore more fully in the next chapter when we unpack the role of personal values in behaviour change.

Our role is to help them slow down, reflect and reframe their perception of reality in a way that reconnects them with what truly matters. This is where Daniel Kahneman's *System 1 and 2* thinking adds power to your coaching. While SDT helps us understand the psychological fuel, System 1 & 2 help us know who's at the wheel.

Remember when I mentioned that the brain's emotional autopilot, System 1, can take over when the road gets foggy? Understanding which part of the brain is behind the steering wheel helps your clients navigate the road forward, especially when the path is unclear or there are obstacles in the way.

So, what exactly is System 1 and System 2?

Imagine your brain is like a car with two drivers that keep switching places:

- System 1 is your intuitive, quick-thinking, emotional autopilot. It's efficient, automatic and heavily shaped by habits, past experiences and emotions.

- System 2 is your slower, logical brain. It's the one that plans, reasons, solves problems and gets tired quickly.

Most of us like to think we're being rational (System 2), but Kahneman's research shows that System 1 is in control most of the time, especially when we're under stress, overwhelmed, or feeling stuck.

'System 1 constructed a story, and System 2 believed it. It happens to all of us.'

Daniel Kahneman

Let's bring this into the Kombi Van metaphor:

- System 1 is riding in the back seat, yelling out shortcuts, *'Just stay home! Avoid the hard stuff! Don't risk it!'*

- System 2 is trying to drive and read the map, but it's easily distracted, and it uses more energy to stay engaged.

If your client is stuck, overwhelmed or repeating self-sabotaging behaviours, chances are System 1 is driving.

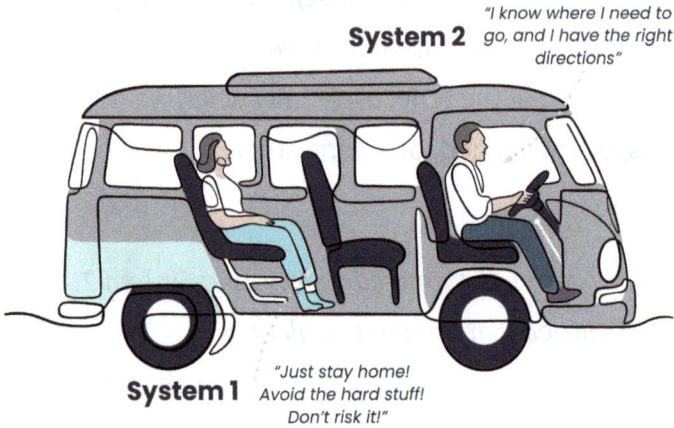

The System 1 & System 2 Kombi Van

What System 1 sounds like in coaching sessions:

System 1 Thinking	What You Might Hear
Emotional, reactive, fear-based	'It's too hard.' 'I always mess this up.'
Habitual responses	'I've always done it this way.'
Avoidance or delay	'I'll start next week.'
Black-and-white thinking	'It's either perfect or pointless.'

System 1 prefers comfort and shortcuts, while System 2 embraces change. When helping clients transition to System 2, the goal is not to silence System 1, but to raise awareness and enable access to System 2 when it's crucial.

Here's how to support the transition:

Slow down the conversation by practising reflective listening and taking intentional pauses.

- Ask things like: *'Let's take a moment. What's really behind that thought?'*

Encourage curiosity with questions instead of commands; System 2 thrives on curiosity.

Try asking:

- *'What would achieving success here look like?'*

- *'Is there another perspective we could consider?'*

Name the Pattern

- *'Would you be open to discussing the thought processes you're currently using?'*

Use Visuals or Metaphors

- Bring back the Kombi Van: *'Who's driving right now, System 1 or System 2?*

Why does this matter in motivation?

When someone says they want to change, but doesn't take action, they're often trapped in System 1 avoidance loops:

- *'Don't try, you'll fail again.'*

- *'Stay safe, stay still.'*

- *'Let's binge-watch something instead.'*

Your job as a coach is to gently interrupt System 1 and nudge them toward conscious, choice-based System 2 thinking.

This is especially true for your clients who may be experiencing rejection, shame, fear of failure, or a long history of being told *'You're not good enough.'* Their System 1 is screaming for safety. You help rewire that loop, one thoughtful conversation at a time.

Practical Tool: The Reframe Shifter

A shifter is a handy tool to have in the boot of your car, especially when you get a flat tyre. I like to carry the Reframe Shifter around in my coaching toolbox, because it's one of the most effective for moving thoughts when they get stuck.

These types of coaching questions activate System 2 thinking:

- *'What's the smallest next step you could take, even if you're unsure?'*

- *'If you had 10% more confidence right now, what would you try?'*

- *'Let's zoom out, how might future-you look back on this?'*

The last question is a reframe, which is arguably one of the most powerful coaching tools you want in your toolkit. In our Job Coach Certification, we deep dive into understanding and working with this tool. This is an overview to help you get started.

Reframing is one of the most potent tools a coach can offer, particularly when clients feel stuck with negative self-talk or unresourceful beliefs. It's not about dismissing their feelings but about helping them see a broader, more empowering perspective. For example, when someone says, *'I've failed too many times to try again,'* a strong reframe could be: *'With every attempt, you've gained more insight. What have these experiences taught you that could help with your next step?'*

This process harmonises well with activating System 2 thinking. Reframing interrupts the automatic, safety-seeking cycle of System 1 and encourages clients to engage in deliberate, reflective thought. It's a gentle yet effective way to guide clients towards curiosity and possibilities without dismissing their lived experiences.

Practical reframing questions include:

1. *'What's another way to look at this situation?'*

2. *'If you were advising a friend facing the same challenge, what would you say?'*

3. *'How might this obstacle be an opportunity in disguise?'*

What's another way to look at this situation?

How might this obstacle be an opportunity in disguise?

If you were advising a friend facing the same challenge, what would you say?

The Reframe Shifter

By reframing, you empower clients to reinterpret their narratives, letting them regain autonomy over their decisions and view their challenges through a lens of growth rather than limitation.

As you integrate these tools into your coaching, remember, it's not about getting it perfect. It's about staying present, staying curious and staying committed to the journey. Before we close this chapter, let's pull off the road for a moment and map out your coaching route using the tools you've just learned.

Activity: Shift gears with STD & System 2 thinking

This activity is designed to show you how to apply Self-Determination Theory and System 1 & 2 thinking in a real coaching scenario, helping you practise identifying motivational drivers, cognitive roadblocks and powerful coaching responses.

Step 1: Choose a client scenario

Consider a current or recent client who appears to be stuck or resistant to change. Write a short paragraph about their situation, including:

- what they say they want

- the actions they are (or aren't) taking

- what you've observed in their behaviour, mindset or language.

Step 2: Map the motivation gears (Self-Determination Theory)

Using the three core needs from SDT, assess what might be missing or under-supported in this client's experience:

Need	What's missing?	How might you support it? (Coaching Strategy or Prompt)
Competence		
Autonomy		
Relatedness		

Step 3: Spot System 1 hijacks

List a few things you've heard this client say that might indicate System 1 thinking is in the driver's seat. Then, reframe those statements or guide them with a System 2-activating question.

System 1 Thought / Belief	Reframe or System 2 Question
e.g. 'I always mess this up.'	'What's one time this *did* go well?'
e.g. 'It's either perfect or pointless.'	'What does 'good enough' look like for today?'

Write your thoughts here:

Step 4: Your Coaching Response

Based on what you uncovered, write 2 – 3 coaching questions you could ask this client in your next session that would:

- build alignment with their intrinsic motivation

- interrupt unhelpful System 1 patterns

- encourage momentum without pressure.

These questions don't have to be perfect; they just need to be honest, curious and designed to open up more space for possibility.

Optional Reflection

This is the space to reflect on Part 1 of this book; your self-awareness is key here.

- Where might your own System 1 assumptions or biases show up when coaching this client?

- What does this exercise teach you about your approach to resistance?

Actionable reflections

- Motivation is created, not imposed. Actual change happens when clients feel aligned, not when they feel pressured.

- Self-Determination Theory reveals that the need for competence, autonomy and relatedness is a universal human need. Meet these needs and motivation naturally follows.

- System 1 and System 2 thinking influence every decision we make. Recognising the patterns and helping clients engage deliberate, reflective thought is a powerful coaching tool.

- Resistance isn't defiance, it's information. It often signals unmet psychological needs or past experiences of shame and failure.

- Reframe, don't rescue. Powerful questions and gentle observations can shift mindsets more effectively than advice or instructions.

- Your clients don't need you to be their engine. They need you to be the one who helps them find the keys, turn the ignition and believe that their

Kombi van can go the distance.

- You're not just coaching behaviour; you're coaching belief, purpose and possibility. The Kombi van is ready. The road is yours to travel. Together, you can drive change.

Conclusion: Turning the kombi van key

Take a moment to consider what it really means to hold space for someone at a crossroads. Your role isn't to jump in the driver's seat, grab the wheel, or push the Kombi from behind. You need to sit in the passenger seat, map in hand, questions at the ready, helping your clients find the confidence to turn the key and choose their own direction

Motivation isn't a switch you flick; it's a spark that needs oxygen. Safety, curiosity, belief and alignment are the fuel that gets the engine humming again. And sometimes, when the road feels uncertain or the engine stalls, your presence alone – calm, steady, and grounded – is what keeps them from giving up on the journey.

Coaching with impact means knowing when to call forward System 2 to quiet the noise of System 1. It's offering a mirror, not a manual. It's reminding them that they're not broken, they just might be running low on fuel, stuck in a rut or doubting whether the road ahead is really meant for them.

When we meet our clients with compassion, insight and belief in their ability to navigate, we hand them back the keys to their own Kombi, and they are ready to go. All we need now is to gather some momentum and create space for sustainable, lasting change. And that's what the final chapter is all about.

Chapter Six

Building Momentum for Lasting Change

Jen was 19 and initially disengaged, reluctantly attending the Bounce Program™ because she was told it was compulsory. She sat at the back of the training room, keeping the hood of her jumper pulled down over her eyes, hugging a large notebook. She avoided conversations with the other participants and contributed very little to group discussions. At times, it seemed as though she wasn't even listening to the discussions, being more content with doodling on random pages in the participant workbook she'd be provided at the start of the program.

I watched her closely over the first couple of days and noticed something interesting during program breaks and downtime. Jen would often retreat to a quiet corner, open her large notebook, and start sketching. Her drawings were intricate and expressive, quietly revealing her inner world. She drew all sorts of images – detailed pictures of places around the world, simple everyday objects, even portraits of the other participants in the room. With a grey lead pencil in hand, she'd fill a page in just minutes with an elaborate image so life-like it left me speechless ...

This final chapter brings together everything we've discussed, offering practical tools and reflective insights to breathe life into your practice and help activate the most vital ingredient for lasting change – hope.

We'll utilise one of the most powerful, future-focused coaching methods, which involves anchoring client strengths and values, applying the GROW model, and helping individuals move beyond merely finding a job to building a meaningful career and life.

This is where transformation begins. Moving beyond the transactional aspects of job placement to the relational, human-focused core of coaching, this process helps people rediscover their worth, connect with what truly matters, and make decisions that last.

Earlier in this book, I encouraged you to consider your values and strengths. That wasn't by chance. The most effective coaching arises from inside-out awareness and understanding who you are, so you can help others discover who they can become.

You are not just a coach. You are a momentum builder, a story shaper and a mirror for your clients to see themselves clearly. In this chapter, we show you how to become that kind of coach, with practical tools and reflective insights to bring your practice to life.

Coach's insight: Jen's breakthrough

When Jen and I started working one-on-one, she admitted she hadn't expected much from the program, but as each day passed, she was surprised at how much it had changed her perspective (and I thought she wasn't listening!). As it turned out, Jen was absorbing every word in her own quietly reflective way. She was thinking about ways to capture what was being said in her sketch book, and even drawing small images in the participant workbook from words the other participants shared.

As we examined her strengths and values, a new clarity emerged. Creativity and self-expression were central to her identity. She realised she wanted to pursue something meaningful, something that allowed her to use her artistic talents and feel that her work made a difference.

That insight changed everything. We used the GROW model to shape her next steps, and she set goals around further study in graphic design and mapped out options to build a portfolio and connect with creative professionals. Her energy shifted. She began to see herself not just as a young person trying to meet expectations, but as someone with a powerful voice and a clear vision.

Her journey wasn't linear, but it was uniquely hers. And it was firmly grounded in her strengths and values.

Jen's story mirrors the same process you went through when examining your strengths and values in Chapter 2. Her breakthrough arose from the precise alignment, not just with a job, but with what energised and mattered to her.

Taking a strengths-based approach

Remember our Kombi van? Explaining System 1 and System 2 thinking? Let's revisit it now, because strengths and values are what keep the Kombi running smoothly.

Think of strengths as the engine, robust, reliable and full of potential. And values? They're the internal GPS, always constantly navigating toward what matters most. When System 1 (your fast, automatic brain) kicks in, it runs best when fuelled by strengths, those tasks and decisions that come naturally and feel energising. When System 2 (your more reflective, deliberate mind) needs to take the wheel, it relies on your values to steer in the right direction, especially when the road gets rough.

So, what happens when you don't know your strengths or can't articulate your values? You stall. You sit at the side of the road, idling with no clear map or motivation to move forward. That's why strengths-based coaching matters.

When we take a strengths-based approach, clients are supported to uncover and embrace their core values, creating a powerful engine for lasting growth, self-belief and alignment. Rather than chasing quick fixes, we tune into what makes people feel alive and purposeful.

Focusing on a client's unique strengths helps them shift gears from self-doubt to self-direction, from stuck to sparked. They start to reframe their challenges as opportunities, clarify what matters, and chart a course that feels not just achievable, but energising.

This type of coaching engages the brain and the body. Clients not only reach their goals, but they also leave with the confidence and clarity to handle any bumps that come up along the way.

In short, strengths-based coaching:

- Builds confidence and motivation

- Boosts self-awareness and sense of purpose

- Aligns actions with values

- Leads to more resilient, empowered decision-making

Just as you explored your values and strengths earlier in this book, your clients deserve the same journey. When you model this work authentically, you hand them the keys to their own Kombi van with an engine that runs on strengths, a map guided by values, and the confidence to navigate every twist and turn ahead.

Using strengths and values to drive change

Strengths-based coaching is a person-centred, future-focused approach grounded in the principles of positive psychology. It involves helping individuals recognise and activate their natural talents and energising behaviours, while also clarifying the values that give their actions meaning.

Strengths are the things people do well and enjoy doing, their natural patterns of thinking, feeling, and behaving, which, when utilised, lead to high levels of performance and satisfaction. According to research by Peterson and Seligman (2004)[23] and further expanded upon by Linley (2008)[24], using one's strengths daily is associated with increased engagement, wellbeing, and life satisfaction. Coaching focused on identifying and activating personal strengths leads to higher engagement, resilience and long-term positive change. The science is clear – when people operate from their strengths, they flourish.

Values are the non-negotiable, deeply held beliefs that shape a person's decisions and define what they care most about. Values provide clarity in decision-making, guide behaviour during uncertainty, and act as a compass for meaningful life and career choices.

In coaching, strengths provide the fuel, and values offer the direction.

As a coach, your role is to help your clients:

- Identify what energises them (strengths)

- Clarify what matters most (values)

- Align actions with both for greater momentum

There are some great tools that you can use to help your clients uncover their strengths. These tools take the guesswork out of strengths discovery, making it a quick and easy process.

Strengths assessments: The VIA Character Survey https://www.viacharacter.org is free; at Bounce, we use the Strengths Profile assessment, which is accredited by Strengths Profilers (https://bounceglobal.net/strength-profiling/).

Reflective questioning: Ask questions such as *'What energises you?'* or *'What do others rely on you for?'*. This is called strengths spotting. We have an activity in this chapter on how to do it.

Observation and affirming feedback: This refers to actively noticing and attentively listening to someone or something, then providing positive reinforcement or validation. Observation involves paying close attention to details, while affirming feedback encourages or confirms good behaviours, ideas, or efforts, fostering motivation and confidence.

When clients know what they're good at and what matters to them, they begin to see themselves differently. They gain a stronger sense of confidence, direction, and hope. For many, just taking the first step toward employment is a breakthrough, one that can open the door to more possibilities down the track. By recognising their strengths and aligning with their values, they begin to believe in their capacity to grow and thrive, not just survive.

This is the essence of the Hope Activation Model, which you explored in Chapter 4, a dynamic, relational process that helps clients move from disengagement to possibility. In that chapter, we explored how hope is not a fixed trait but a state that can be cultivated through human connection, relational energy and intentional coaching. One of the most powerful ways to spark this hope is by helping clients uncover their strengths and values. When they connect to what energises them and align it with what truly matters, they begin to experience a sense of agency, the belief that they can take meaningful steps toward their goals. My Bounce Program participant, Jen, was in this space – once we identified her strengths and aligned them with her value of creativity, we were able to shift gears and change direction. Strengths-based coaching activates this internal shift. It's how we turn insight into action, and action into momentum.

You might recognise parts of this approach from your own journey in Chapter 2. You reflected deeply on what energises you and what you can no longer ignore. These same questions now become the tools you offer your clients.

Activity: Strengths spotting

This powerful coaching activity uses appreciative inquiry to help clients become aware of the strengths others see in them. It builds confidence, enhances self-awareness and ignites motivation.

Create the container. Start with a grounding chat. Ask your client to reflect on a time when they felt energised, proud or accomplished. Help them get into a mindset of openness and curiosity.

Use your coach lens. As they talk, listen deeply. Notice the language they use, their body language, and any moments where they appear to be genuinely engaged. Jot down the strengths you hear or observe, like resilience, humour, empathy and problem-solving.

Give strength-based feedback. Reflect back what you notice:

- *'When you talked about supporting your friend through that situation, I saw so much compassion and calm. Those are incredible strengths.'*

- *'You lit up when you described organising that event. I wonder if structure and leadership are strengths for you?'*

Invite their insights. Ask:

- *Which of these strengths feels most true to you?'*

- *'Which ones do you enjoy using the most?'*

- *'Which ones surprise you?'*

Anchor to action. Explore how they might apply one of these strengths to a current goal or challenge:

- *'How could your strength in empathy support you during a job interview?' 'What would change if you led with your creativity in this next step?'*

This is a strengths mirror, a way of highlighting what is already working, worthy and present in the client. It builds hope and belief, one insight at a time.

Exploring their values

If strengths are the engine that propels the Kombi
forward, values are the compass, the internal GPS that
keeps your client on a path that feels meaningful.
Values guide every important decision we make, often
without us realising it. When clients are out of alignment
with their values, they may feel frustrated, stuck,
or disconnected, even if they've achieved something
externally.

Helping clients identify and understand their values
reconnects them to what matters most, providing
context for their strengths and clarifying the purpose
behind their actions.

Values are the deeply held principles or beliefs that
give meaning to our lives. They're not goals, they're
the emotional drivers behind our goals. For clients who
have faced long-term unemployment or experienced
disadvantage, values may centre around stability, dignity
and contribution.

For example:

- A client might say they want a job with regular
  hours; underneath that could be a deep value for

predictability, routine or family responsibility.

- Another client may resist roles that involve high pressure or criticism; their underlying value may be psychological safety or respect.

- Someone may long to work in a job where they're helping others, because they value kindness, connection or community impact.

When clients understand their values, even if they've never named them before, it empowers them to see why certain choices feel energising and others feel draining. They begin to trust themselves more, even after a long period of feeling judged, overlooked, or stuck. With alignment comes clarity, confidence and a renewed sense of direction.

Values are the deeply held principles or beliefs that give meaning to our lives. They're not goals, they're the emotional drivers behind our goals. For example, a client may want a steady job, but it's not just about the income. It may be about the value of security or responsibility. Another may resist certain roles not because of the tasks, but because the job clashes with their value of creativity or freedom.

When clients understand their values, they're more likely to make decisions that align with their identity. And with alignment comes energy, confidence and clarity.

Activity: Values discovery

Use this coaching sequence to help your client uncover their core values:

Invite your client to reflect:

- *'Tell me about a time when you felt proud of something you did.'*

- *'What made that moment meaningful?'*

- *'What was important to you in that experience?'*

Look for themes. As they speak, listen for emotional language and key drivers, such as words like fairness, growth, connection or impact.

Name the value. Reflect back what you hear:

- *'It sounds like making a difference is really important to you.'*

- *'You mentioned how you loved feeling independent – that could be a core value.'*

Check in. Ask:

- *'Does that value feel true for you?'*

- *'What does that value give you when it's being honoured?'*

- *'What happens when that value is not met?'*

Align with goals. Once a few core values are identified, ask:

- *'How can we make sure your next steps reflect this value?'*

- *'What kind of work or environment would allow you to express this value more often?'*

Helping clients see how their values and strengths work together lays the foundation for sustained confidence and action. This clarity also reinforces the Hope Activation Model introduced earlier, because when clients feel seen, understood and aligned with what truly matters, their sense of agency expands.

Once a client has insight into what energises them and what matters most, we need a practical way to help them take action. That's where the GROW model comes in. It offers a clear, supportive structure to guide clients from reflection to real-world momentum.

Just as the Hope Activation Model taught us that agency grows through connection and alignment, strengths-based coaching provides the fuel. When clients name what energises them and clarify what they care most about, they begin to see real, tangible possibilities ahead. This is the spark that sets hope in motion.

Applying the GROW Coaching Model

The GROW Model is a simple model for coaching conversations. It helps clients move from self-reflection to action in a way that feels supportive, clear, and achievable. Initially developed by Sir John Whitmore (2002), the GROW Model[25] stands for:

GOAL > REALITY > OPTIONS > WAY FORWARD

It's a great tool to use once a client has gained insight into their strengths and values. By plugging those insights into the GROW process, you help them build momentum and take meaningful steps toward change.

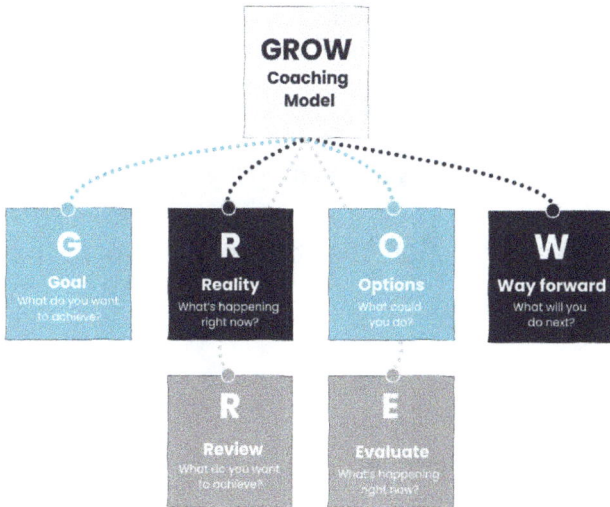

The Grow Coaching Model

Here's how to use it in a one-on-one coaching conversation:

G – Goal = *'What do you want to achieve?'*

Ask your client to set a meaningful and personal goal, not just one they think you want to hear. It could be:

- *'I want to feel confident enough to apply for a job again.'*

- *'I want to find a job where I feel respected and safe.'*

Make sure the goal is specific, measurable, and aligned with their values. This is not just about outcomes, it's about who they want to be.

R – Reality = *'What's happening right now?'*

Help the client explore their current situation without judgment:

- *'I haven't worked in two years.'*

- *I don't have a resume anymore.'*

- *'I feel anxious every time I think about interviews.'*

Hold space for honesty. Acknowledge the barriers but also look for moments of strength and resourcefulness that they may not have noticed.

O – Options = *'What could you do?'*

Now, shift gears into possibility. Build from their strengths and values:

- *'You said you're good with people, what roles could use that strength?'*

- *'If respect and routine are important to you, what kind of workplace would match that?'*

- *'What's one small step you could take this week to move forward?'*

Avoid rushing into problem-solving. Let them explore different pathways and choose what feels realistic and energising.

W – Way Forward = *'What will you do next?'*

This final stage is about commitment and accountability:

- *'What's the very next step you'll take?'*

- *'When will you do it?'*

- *'How will you keep going if it gets hard?'*

Tie their action to their values and identity. That connection becomes the fuel to keep going when motivation dips.

'You said independence matters to you. How will doing this next step bring you closer to that?'

The GROW Model aligns beautifully with the Hope Activation Model. When clients clarify what matters to them (their values), understand what makes them feel strong (their strengths), and take guided, values-aligned action (GROW), they increase their sense of agency, one of the essential conditions for hope.

When you coach using this model, you're not just helping someone take action. You're helping them believe in the person they are becoming.

Take Amina, a single mum in her early 40's who hadn't worked in nearly a decade. During coaching, she identified that her top strengths were planning and compassion. Her core value? Stability for her kids. Using GROW, she set a goal to apply for admin roles in local schools. That connection between values, strengths, and direction helped her move forward, one small, hopeful step at a time.

But coaching doesn't stop at setting goals and moving forward. Real life brings obstacles, setbacks, and unexpected turns. That's why Australian coaching psychologist Anthony Grant proposed an evolution of the model known as REGROW[26]. This version keeps the original steps of GROW but adds two important elements:

R – Review: pausing to reflect on progress, celebrate wins and acknowledge challenges.

E – Evaluate: assessing what's working, what isn't and adjusting the approach.

Together, these additions turn a single coaching conversation into a cycle of growth. REGROW reinforces that change is rarely linear, focusing on trying, learning and trying again. For clients like Amina, this means every step (even the hard ones) becomes part of building confidence and sustaining hope.

Practical Tool: GROW Coaching Planner

Use this planner to structure a one-on-one coaching conversation using the GROW model. Let it guide the session naturally, building clarity, confidence and commitment along the way.

G – GOAL = What do you want to achieve?

☐ What's important to you right now?

☐ What would success look like?

☐ How will you know you've achieved it?

Coach Notes:

R – REALITY = What's happening right now?

☐ What's your current situation?

☐ What's working well?

☐ What are the obstacles?

☐ What strengths or resources do you already have?

Coach Notes:

O – OPTIONS = What could you do?

☐ What are the possible paths forward?

☐ What have you tried already?

☐ Who could help you?

☐ What ideas feel most realistic and energising?

Coach Notes:

W – WAY FORWARD = What will you do next?

☐ What's your next step?

☐ When will you take it?

☐ What might get in the way?

☐ How will you stay on track?

☐ How does this action align with your values?

```
Coach Notes:


```

Come back to strengths and values at every stage, as they are your client's internal compass. Reflect back what you hear and affirm what you see. Your presence matters as much as your questions.

Actionable reflections

- Strengths are the engine. They energise clients, boost confidence and help them move forward with clarity and resilience. When clients understand their strengths, they feel more capable of handling challenges and creating opportunities.

- Values are the compass. Values guide decision-making and help clients align their actions with what matters most to them. This internal alignment creates motivation and meaning, especially for clients who've felt stuck or lost.

- Hope is activated through alignment. When strengths and values are identified and integrated into coaching conversations, clients gain agency, a core ingredient of hope. This ties directly to the Hope Activation Model you learned earlier in the book.

- Strengths-based coaching builds self-awareness. Clients see themselves not through a deficit lens, but as capable, resilient, and resourceful human beings. This mindset shift is foundational to long-term change.

- The GROW Model turns insight into action. Once strengths and values are explored, GROW provides the structure to guide clients from reflection to real-world steps that feel achievable and energising.

- Small steps matter. For many clients, just reconnecting with hope, confidence and purpose is a significant win. Celebrate those milestones. Honour their journey.

- You are a co-pilot. You don't need to have all the answers. Your role is to walk alongside, listen deeply, reflect honestly and guide gently, offering just enough structure for them to take the wheel of their own Kombi van.

Conclusion: Bringing it all together

The transformative power of strengths-based coaching lies in the intentional integration of strengths and values, which becomes the catalyst for clarity, agency and hope. By focusing on strengths as energisers and values as guiding principles, coaches empower clients to approach challenges with confidence and purpose.

The REGROW Model provides a bridge from reflection to action, ensuring that new insights translate into meaningful steps forward. Progress is often found in small, celebrated milestones, and the coach's role is to serve as a supportive co-pilot, offering both structure and space for clients to drive their own growth.

Ultimately, this approach fosters self-awareness, resilience and a hopeful mindset, reminding clients that positive change is not only possible, but also within their grasp.

Strengths-based coaching is not just a method. It's a mindset. And when you coach this way, you not only help your clients get moving, but you also help them believe that a better future is possible.

Onward

A New Beginning Beyond the Final Page ...

Take a moment to breathe deeply and reflect on everything you've gained.

This book is a catalyst for change within yourself and in the lives of those you support. It offers guidance, reflection and a powerful reminder that transformation starts from within.

We've journeyed together through self-awareness, emotional intelligence, strengths and values. We explored how to ignite hope, build trust and stand beside people who feel stuck or invisible. You learned the psychology of motivation, unlocked the mysteries of the human mind and discovered how curiosity can break old habits and create new possibilities.

Now, you have the tools to turn good intentions into meaningful impact.

But here's the truth: the tools aren't the magic ingredient. You are.

Your presence. Your energy. Your belief in someone who hasn't yet learned to believe in themselves.

You are the quiet but powerful force that says, *'I see you. I believe in you. And I'll walk with you every step of the way.'*

We've talked about coaching journeys and Kombi vans; here's one last image for you: a convoy. Picture all the people you've coached – past, present, and future. Each person behind the wheel of their own Kombi van. Some are stalled, some are idling, and others are already cruising down the road. And there you are, not driving for them or shouting directions, but travelling beside them. You're the guide who cheers them on during steep climbs, shares your map when the roads are foggy, and celebrates each small victory.

You are a spark that sets change in motion. You ignite hope. You build momentum for lasting transformation.

When you show up with authenticity and compassion, you help people find more than just jobs; you help them rediscover their worth, reclaim their agency and believe that something better is possible. That's the kind of coach the world needs. That's the kind of coach you've become.

So, dive back into your work with fresh eyes, an open heart, and a toolkit ready to create change. Hold space for others with care and wisdom. Ask the questions that uncover new paths. And always remember this: your energy inspires, your belief empowers and your presence matters more than you know.

Let's keep driving change together.

Gratitude

Writing this book has been both a deeply personal journey and a professional milestone. I could never have done it alone.

First, to the incredible job coaches, consultants and leaders I've had the privilege of working with over the years, you are the heart of this book. Your passion, persistence and dedication to helping people find their place in the world of work have been my constant inspiration. Every story, insight and idea here has been shaped by the conversations we've had and the journeys we've shared.

To the job seekers themselves – thank you for your courage, honesty and trust. Your resilience in the face of challenge is the reason this work matters. It has been an honour to walk beside you and to witness the transformations that happen when hope and opportunity align.

I want to acknowledge my Bounce Global team. You have believed in this vision, carried it forward and pushed me to keep creating. A special thank you to Donna Wardlaw, who has been my steady collaborator, sounding board and friend on this book journey.

To my mentors, colleagues and partners across the employment services sector in Australia and around the world, thank you for your encouragement and for challenging me to think bigger, dig deeper and stay true to the purpose of this work.

To my family, thank you for your patience, love and unwavering support. You have kept me grounded and reminded me why this work matters beyond the page.

Finally, to every reader who picks up this book: thank you. By investing in your own growth as a coach or consultant, you are helping to create more resilient, hopeful pathways for the people you serve. And that is work worth celebrating.

References

1. Snyder, C. R., Rand, K. L., & Sigmon, D. R. (2002). Hope theory: A member of the positive psychology family. In C. R. Snyder & S. J. Lopez (Eds.), *Handbook of positive psychology* (pp. 257–276). Oxford University Press.

2. Goleman, D. Working with Emotional Intelligence (1998) and The Emotionally Intelligent Leader (2019).

3. https://www.talentsmarteq.com/media/uploads/pdfs/Business_Case_For_Emotional_Intelligence.pdf

4. DiGirolamo, J.A. and Tkach, J.T., Reflective Practice for Coaches and Clients: An Integrated Model for Learning, Alicia M. Hullinger, Lexington, USA.

5. Schön, D. (1983). The Reflective Practitioner: How Professionals Think in Action. London: Temple Smith.

6. Carden, J., Jones, R.J. & Passmore, J. An exploration of the role of coach training in developing self-awareness: a mixed methods study. Curr Psychol 42, 6164–6178 (2023)

7. Fredrickson-Danner-Snowdon-2003-The-Value-of-Positive-Emotions

8. Bloom, P. (2016). *Against empathy: the case for rational compassion.* First edition. Ecco, an imprint of Harper Collins Publishers.

9. Bloom, P. (2016). *Against empathy: the case for rational compassion.* First edition. Ecco, an imprint of Harper Collins Publishers.

10. Owens, B. P., & Patterson, K. (2013). Relational energy at work: Implications for job engagement and job performance. Journal of Applied Psychology, 101(1), 35–49.

11. Baker, W. E. (2019). Emotional energy, relational energy, and organizational energy: Toward a multilevel model. Annual Review of Organizational Psychology and Organizational Behavior, 6, 373–393.

12. Sumpter, D. M., & Gibson, C. B. (2022). Riding the wave to recovery: Relational energy as an HR managerial resource for employees during crisis recovery. Human Resource Management, 62(4), 581–613.

13. Owens, B. P., Baker, W. E., Sumpter, D. M., & Cameron, K. S. (2016). Relational energy at work: Implications for job engagement and job performance. Journal of Applied Psychology, 101(1), 35–49.

14. Biswas-Diener, R., & van Nieuwerburgh, C. (2024). Radical Listening: The Art of True Connection. Open University Press.

15. Fowkes, L., & O'Sullivan, S. (2023). 'You're not a robot': Burnout and emotional labour among employment services workers. The Australian Journal of Social Issues, 58(2), 208–225.

16. Snyder, C. R., Rand, K. L., & Sigmon, D. R. (2002). Hope theory: A member of the positive psychology family. In C. R. Snyder & S. J. Lopez (Eds.), *Handbook of positive psychology* (pp. 257–276). Oxford University Press.

17. Goleman, D. and Boyatzis, R., 2006. Emotional intelligence: The new science of human relationships.

18. Ryan, R. M., & Deci, E. L. (2000). Self-determination theory and the facilitation of intrinsic motivation, social development, and well-being. *American Psychologist, 55*(1), 68–78. https://doi.org/10.1037/0003-066X.55.1.68

19. Deci, E. L., & Ryan, R. M. (1985). *Intrinsic Motivation and Self-Determination in Human Behavior*. New York: Plenum Press.

20. Kahneman, D. (2013). *Thinking, fast and slow.* First paperback edition. Farrar, Straus and Giroux.

21. Deci, E. L., & Ryan, R. M. (1985). *Intrinsic Motivation and Self-Determination in Human Behavior*. New York: Plenum Press.

22. Sykes, C., 2023. How Australia's employment services system fails jobseekers: Insights from self-determination theory. *Australian Journal of Labour Economics, 26*(1), pp.84-113.

23. Peterson, C., & Seligman, M. E. P. (2004). Character Strengths and Virtues: A Handbook and Classification. Oxford University Press.

24. Linley, A. (2008). Average to A+: Realising Strengths in Yourself and Others. CAPP Press.

25. Whitmore, J. (2002). Coaching for Performance. Nicholas Brealey Publishing.

26. Grant, A. M. (2011). Is it time to REGROW the GROW model? Issues related to teaching coaching session structures. Coaching: An International Journal of Theory, Research and Practice.

About the Author
Maria Smith

Maria Smith is an award-winning facilitator, speaker and changemaker dedicated to transforming the way people connect, learn and thrive – especially in the employment services sector. As the Founder and Creative Director of Bounce Global, Maria has worked with thousands of job coaches, consultants and employment professionals across Australia and around the world, helping them build the confidence, mindset and resilience to create lasting impact.

Maria holds a Master of Applied Positive Psychology from the University of Melbourne, where her research focused on activating hope and building trust in complex systems. With a background that spans theatre, community development and neuroscience-informed coaching, she brings a rare blend of heart, science and story to everything she does.

She is best known for pioneering strengths-based approaches to human services training, including the Bounce Program™ and Job Coach Certification. Maria's methods are trusted by government departments, disability employment services and global partners seeking to rehumanise systems and empower the people within them.

Maria's third book, *Building Resilient Pathways*, is a deeply practical, soulfully written guide to coaching with self-awareness, trust and authentic human connection.

To find out more about Maria's training, resources and programs, head to:

www.bounceglobal.net or email info@bounceglobal.net

9 781923 008458